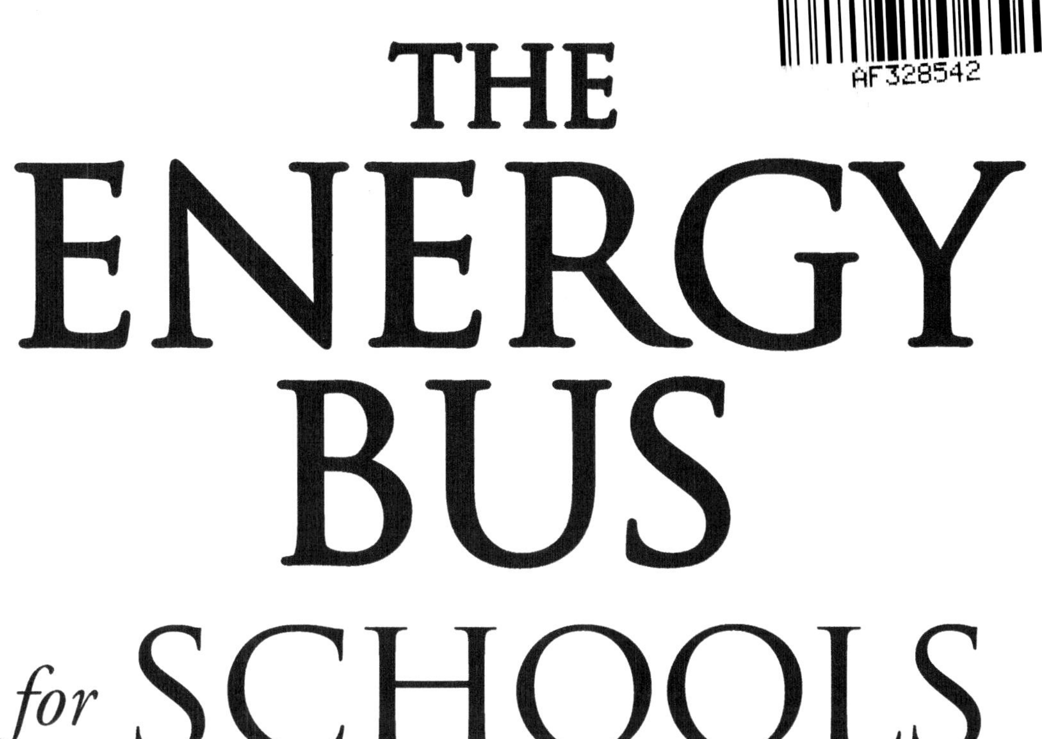

THE ENERGY BUS

BUS

for SCHOOLS

FIELD GUIDE

Praise for *The Energy Bus for Schools*

"*The Energy Bus for Schools* is an empowering and transformative guide that transcends the boundaries of conventional education. Filled with relatable insights and actionable steps, it's a game-changer for schools, teachers, and anyone invested in making a positive impact. A must-read if you are seeking to amplify leadership, inspire minds, and create a legacy that truly matters."

—**Jessica Holsman,** bestselling author and founder of *Study With Jess*

"*The Energy Bus for Schools* provides a clear roadmap for establishing and maintaining a positive school culture that's easy to follow and simple to implement! Gordon and Van Allan give suggestions, tips, and examples that will guide educational leaders through the process for building and improving school culture one step at a time in order to increase success for all stakeholders, including staff members, students, and communities."

—**Michelle Emerson,** author of *First Class Teaching*

"At a time when educators are feeling particularly tested, *The Energy Bus for Schools* is the perfect companion to its widely read predecessor. Jon Gordon and Dr. Jim Van Allan share a collection of motivating and often moving stories from schools across the country to support educators as we reframe how we 'do school' moving forward."

—**Donna Hayward,** NASSP 2023 National Principal of the Year

"Jim Van Allan and Jon Gordon's *The Energy Bus for Schools* is exactly the message I needed to organize my thoughts and improve my approach in overcoming negativity and adversity that are often encountered in the workplace. The tools learned in this book will assist me in building a positive culture, where the staff can reach our school goals, despite any obstacles that may come our way."

—**Adam Lane,** NASSP 2022 Florida Principal of the Year

"Calling all educators! *The Energy Bus for Schools* is a game-changer for educators seeking to create a positive and unified school culture. Jon and Jim have compiled powerful examples from schools nationwide, providing transformative strategies that truly work. With real stories, turn-key strategies, and research-based insights, this invaluable resource will help you make a lasting positive impact on your school community!"

—**Dr. David Arencibia,** National Principal of the Year
Finalist and Texas Principal of the Year

THE ENERGY BUS
BUS
for SCHOOLS

FIELD GUIDE

JON GORDON

Bestselling Author of *The Energy Bus*

DR. JIM VAN ALLAN

President, Energy Bus for Schools

WILEY

Published by John Wiley & Sons, Inc., Hoboken, New Jersey.
Published simultaneously in Canada.

Library of Congress Cataloging-in-Publication Data is Available:

ISBN: 9781394352883 (Paperback)
ISBN: 9781394352890 (ePub)
ISBN: 9781394352906 (ePDF)

COVER DESIGN: PAUL MCCARTHY
COVER ART: © ISCHNEIDER/GETTY IMAGES

Contents

The Case for a Positive School Culture

Jon Gordon and I have been immensely influenced by teachers, administrators, and schools. Jon Gordon, through his educational experience on Long Island, New York, and Dr. Jim Van Allan, from Palm Harbor, Florida, can point to specific teachers, schools, and moments that shaped our ways of thinking. These experiences developed us into positive leaders and planted seeds for us to become speakers later in life. We also both benefited from amazing school environments and teachers who loved, supported, challenged, and valued us. We are the men, fathers, husbands, and speakers we are today because of the inspiring school leaders, supportive staff, and empowering culture that laid the foundation for our growth.

Teaching and leading schools can sometimes be thankless jobs, especially as students graduate and move on with their lives. However, as students journey through life, they will inevitably look back and remember the educators that influenced, inspired, and impacted them.

The key is to give these current students an experience that will last a lifetime—one so powerful and so positive that they will want to re-create it for their own children. When students have their own families, they will try to emulate experiences and environments they had growing up or run from them. It's that simple. We lean into good thoughts and experiences and shy away from others. There is no greater responsibility for a parent than to protect and love their children. One way they can do this is through selecting a school that will partner with them to accomplish this.

This field guide offers the perfect opportunity to think about your school culture and your role, responsibilities, and ability to impact others. Recent studies in the *Educational Administration* journal show how important it is to create a positive workplace culture that keeps employees engaged and boosts morale. When staff feel supported, their well-being improves, which leads to better results for students. We created this field guide to make this a reality. Our current and future students need educators who are motivated and passionate and equipped to deal with the challenges surrounding the ever-changing field of education.

A positive school culture is the heartbeat of every thriving campus. When culture is strong, everything else finds its rhythm and rises with it. Vision, mission, and strategy cannot be effectively implemented and lived unless there is a culture in place that values collaboration, trust, and a shared commitment to growth and well-being. When a school knows what they stand for and has a positive and relationship-driven culture, they will hire people who reflect those attributes. As schools grow, and times change, even the best and most engaged schools have to constantly assess their culture. This field guide represents an opportunity to do just that.

The positive examples and case studies featured in this field guide will inspire you to look inward and develop a strong culture that will lower attrition rates and increase student and staff engagement. A positive culture does not happen by accident. It takes a group of ambitious and motivated people who share a common language and a love for the profession working toward the same goal. Together, you have the power to create something extraordinary because a positive culture isn't just built; it's lived every day through purpose, passion, and unwavering belief in what's possible.

Exploring *The Energy Bus for Schools Field Guide*

Since the original book, *The Energy Bus,* came out in 2007, it has consistently been a bestseller. Schools and educators still gravitate toward that book as an effective tool to become more positive and overcome negativity. As *The Energy Bus* grew in popularity, there were requests for more resources from schools.

This led us to create The Energy Bus for Schools Certified program. It is a simple and transformative program that helps schools bring to life the concepts in *The Energy Bus*. It provides a blueprint and framework to energize teachers and empower students through classroom activities, monthly coaching, and staff development resources.

As the Certified Energy Bus for Schools program expanded around the country and across the world, we heard many incredible stories of transformation and growth as

The Case for a Positive School Culture

schools drove their Energy Buses. We wanted to share these stories and case studies. This led us to write *The Energy Bus for Schools* book in 2024, a much-anticipated follow-up to the original *The Energy Bus* book from 2007. Schools can now dive into both books, experiencing the original fable before learning and implementing specific strategies to inspire your school.

Enter this field guide, a valuable resource that is intended to be completed after reading *The Energy Bus for Schools* book. It equips and empowers educators to bring the concepts from the book to life in an engaging and collaborative format.

Who Should Use This Field Guide?

This field guide is designed for all educators connected to a school or district, including teachers, staff members, administrators, district-level employees, and classified staff. It can be used individually, in professional learning communities (PLCs), as part of staff professional development, or even during book club discussions. It serves as a companion to *The Energy Bus for Schools*.

Here are a few ways schools can utilize this guide effectively: One option is to introduce it at the beginning of the school year and complete one or two principles at a time during professional development days before students return to campus. Also, schools can implement it gradually by incorporating it into staff meetings throughout the fall semester. Additionally, smaller groups, such as PLCs, can work through the guide one principle at a time. Be sure to tailor this guide to align with your school's unique calendar and needs.

If your school staff is seeking to empower one another, strengthen relationships, and reflect on individual and collective well-being, this field guide will support your journey. It is designed to challenge educators while fostering collaboration and meaningful conversations about school culture. The guide follows the core principles outlined in *The Energy Bus for Schools* to help bring these concepts to life in an actionable way.

As you develop ideas from this field guide, be sure to utilize your Positive Culture team to help turn the ideas into reality (see Chapter 2, "Build a Positive Culture"). This team will help to organize people, ideas, and initiatives and delegate responsibility and monitor progress.

The Case for a Positive School Culture

These principles, inspired by the original *The Energy Bus* book, are tailored to provide schools and educators with streamlined content that makes building a positive school culture effective and accessible.

Invite Others on the Bus

Build a Positive Culture

Fuel Your Ride with Positive Energy

Love Your Passengers

Transform Negativity

Refuel, Reenergize, and Refocus with Purpose

Create a Fleet of Bus Drivers

We know you will enjoy the ride!

Chapter 1

Invite Others on the Bus and Share the Vision

As a school, who you are and what you stand for are central to building a positive culture. When these elements are clear, they form the foundation for everything you hope to accomplish. A few years back, I heard from a school in Colorado that had gone through several principal changes in a short period of time. None of the previous leaders had worked with the staff to define the school's vision or mission. Left without direction, the staff gradually drifted apart, despite working in a small building. They needed help. They needed an identity.

The newly hired principal, determined to stay and make a difference, reached out after reading *The Energy Bus*. His one request: a professional development session focused solely on vision. During our in-person visit, we spent three hours with the entire staff defining their core values and crafting a shared vision and mission. We posted potential statements around the room for discussion and voted. After years of silence, the staff eagerly participated. By the end of the session, they collectively established their guiding principles and a clear path forward. Years later, that school is thriving because they built a shared mission and identity. Vision provides a unifying sense of purpose, built through collaboration and shared commitment.

This process isn't just theoretical; it's actionable. At a different school, one principal even took the concept literally: She invited her staff onto a school bus, drove through students' neighborhoods, and handed out treats and well-wishes. Her vision was to create open, positive relationships, and this symbolic gesture brought her team and community closer.

Being on the Energy Bus means working toward a shared goal of building a dynamic, positive school environment. It all starts with defining a vision and inviting others to join the journey. School leaders must extend that invitation, and staff must see it as an opportunity to lead, collaborate, and shape the future together.

Even those who aren't in a school or district leadership role should cultivate the ambition to create a strategic vision for their life, family, classroom, or workspace. Sharing these plans with students, parents, and colleagues helps foster transparency, collaboration, and a shared sense of purpose. When others see your vision in action, it can inspire them to pursue their own goals and contribute to a positive, united environment.

It's time to get on the Energy Bus and plot a course ahead.

Connection Builders

Understand

Why is it so important to invite others to join your "bus" when sharing your vision?

____

____

____

____

____

Reflect

Have you ever been inspired to join someone else's vision? What inspired you to get involved?

____

____

____

____

____

Consider the following three areas: *Personal, Classroom, School.*

Write a one-sentence vision statement for each area. Your statements should be clear, specific, and action-oriented, reflecting what you want each area to look and feel like. If you are a school administrator, substitute "classroom" with your leadership role. Please discuss with your groups.

1. Personal

2. Classroom (or Leadership Role)

3. School

Invite Others on the Bus and Share the Vision

Apply

Now that you have written down and discussed your vision for three different areas, it's time to focus on the action component. First, for the same three areas, brainstorm one or two immediate action items that can be started right away.

Area	Immediate Action Items
Personal	__________________________
	__________________________
	__________________________
Classroom	__________________________
	__________________________
	__________________________
School	__________________________
	__________________________
	__________________________

One Word

Now that everyone has a clear vision for the road ahead, it is time to simplify things. While vision statements are essential to move forward in the right direction, it is also helpful to have a simple reminder of our vision by using One Word. This concept involves reflecting on your previously written vision statements and attaching one word to capture the essence of the information. For this activity, you will use your personal vision statement. Reread your vision statement and action items and pick One Word that would encompass your personal vision. When ready, write it in the designated area along with your statement on why you chose that word. Please share with your group or have various educators stand up to share with everyone. The entire group should hold up their One Words for all to see.

Invite Others on the Bus and Share the Vision

Team Connection

Whom do you need to invite on your bus? Using your three areas of life, identify individuals you can invite to be part of your vision. You can write their names, roles, or something else to identify them.

Area	People
Personal	
Classroom	
School	

The Energy Bus for Schools Field Guide

Team-Building Activities

1. Self-Reflection

Think about your teaching or leadership style. Everyone has a style that defines them as an educator. In groups of four to six people, participants should define their teaching or leadership style with a few keywords. Be sure to elaborate on the *why* behind the style and share both the key words and added context with the people in your group. Feel free to use some space here to brainstorm:

Teaching/Leadership Style

Why?

Invite Others on the Bus and Share the Vision

In these same small groups, write and discuss one thing each person wants to do differently this school year. Focus on why each person feels the need for change and what are their anticipated results. For example, during one Energy Bus for Schools workshop, a teacher mentioned to me she wanted to change up the morning routine with her students. She felt like just jumping into the material with high school students was not as effective and wanted to try mini-icebreakers or targeted conversation to warm up the class.

In addition, move the conversation to one thing each person wants to be more consistent with, something they want to do more. Not every routine has to be changed each year and there may be areas that school leaders and teachers need to lean into more. In a similar workshop for staff, one teacher said she need to be more consistent with saying hello to and interacting with people in the halls. As each person shares, listen and learn and grow together. Jot some notes down in the space that follows.

Different

____

____

____

____

____

____

Consistent

____

____

____

____

____

____

2. Fears

It's natural to feel a little anxious when planning for the future, whether it's near or far, but it's also the first step toward exciting possibilities. Whether you complete this field guide midyear or at the beginning of the school year, everyone has a fear or two about their situation. Ask people to get into groups of four to six people and discuss a fear each person has about the school year. Many times we do not talk about our fears and they can get worse through overthinking. Allow each person time to share and discuss where their school-related fears originate. Use this group time to encourage and lift everyone up. Each person should feel heard and valued. Feel free to use the space below to jot down any keywords that resonate with you or capture key ideas you want to remember.

____

____

____

____

____

____

____

____

____

____

____

____

____

Invite Others on the Bus and Share the Vision

3. Positive Visualization

Studies have shown that positive visualization activates the same neural pathways in the brain as actual physical practice. It helps focus the mind, reduce anxiety, and build confidence by mentally rehearsing success. Whenever you are working on this field guide, you hold the opportunity to envision success and take the next step toward it. In groups, take time to brainstorm and list as many successes as you can envision achieving this year. Be sure to encourage and celebrate with others as they share.

Use this space to list successes you are visualizing this school year:

The Energy Bus for Schools Field Guide

4. The Vision Bus

This team-building activity will build upon the vision activities earlier in this chapter. Hang flipchart paper in front of the room. Refer back to the school vision statements you created earlier. Choose a few key words from several people's visions and write them on the flipchart paper. Next, collaborate and analyze what has been written on the flipchart paper and decide on one collective vision for the school.

Have a large school bus drawn on butcher paper or another type of paper hanging in the room. Ask some creative people to decorate the bus. The agreed-upon collective vision should be written on the school bus.

School leaders can go to https://www.theenergybus.com/tickets.html and download bus tickets from the website. Hand these out to all staff members. This is the chance for school leaders to invite their staff onto the bus! Each staff member should sign their ticket and write their name on the school bus while turning in their ticket to the principal. Additionally, staff members can tape their tickets to the large bus with their signed names.

Prominently display the bus around campus for community members, parents, and students to see. This collective vision will give the school a sense of identity, direction, and belonging for all. Each person contributed to the vision, accepted their ticket on the bus, and is now accountable to making the vision a reality by living it.

Invite Others on the Bus and Share the Vision

Case Study: Building a Shared Vision Through Collaboration

Southeastern Regional Vocational Technical High School

Creating a shared vision within a school district requires collaboration from all stakeholders. At Southeastern Regional Vocational Technical High School in Massachusetts, the process began with developing a strategic plan that involved school committee members, administrators, teachers, students, and caregivers. The objective was to craft a unified vision and mission while establishing actionable goals for the next three years.

One key aspect of creating and sharing the school's vision was a strong commitment to staff engagement, which began with fostering open communication and promoting a collaborative mindset. Regular meetings with vocational programs and supervisors provided meaningful opportunities to discuss achievements, challenges, future goals, and professional development needs. These conversations helped identify and address barriers, ensuring that faculty members felt supported and valued. As part of this process, meetings were held with 20 vocational programs, with additional sessions scheduled for academic departments and paraprofessionals. This intentional approach ensured that staff perspectives were actively heard and considered in decision-making.

The school ultimately developed a comprehensive and collaborative vision, one shaped by the voices and input of its educators. Staff were not only invited to contribute to the vision, but also encouraged to embrace it and bring it to life in their daily work. By involving all stakeholders in the process, the school created a shared vision that reflects the collective values, aspirations, and commitment of the entire school community.

Staff at Southeastern Regional Vocational Technical High School serve brunch to other staff members. They truly have a collaborative spirit around creating a positive vision.

Invite Others on the Bus and Share the Vision

 # Best Practices and Main Takeaways

- **Define a clear vision through collaboration.** A shared vision creates a sense of identity, purpose, and direction. Involving all stakeholders in defining core values and vision and mission statements fosters commitment and collective ownership.

- **Build relationships through symbolic actions.** Actions like visiting students' neighborhoods or creating symbolic activities help strengthen relationships among staff, students, and the community, reinforcing a positive culture.

- **Engage staff in vision creation and accountability.** Actively involving staff in creating a collective vision ensures everyone feels heard and responsible for implementing the vision. Tools like signed bus tickets can symbolize this shared accountability.

- **Foster open communication and recognition.** Regular meetings, honest conversations, and meaningful appreciation efforts strengthen staff engagement and sustain a positive school culture.

- **Practice positive visualization and team-building.** Activities like brainstorming successes, envisioning future achievements, and conducting reflective exercises help staff align with the school's vision while promoting a supportive environment.

Personal Reflection

How could the new knowledge, skills, and strategies from this section impact your campus and your role?

____

____

____

____

Build a Positive Culture

The previous section helped you to focus on the vision defining, writing, and implementation process. It brought to life the fact that vision and mission give a school a sense of identity. When team members contribute to the vision, it gives them a sense of community and belonging. There is a caveat, though. Thomas Edison said it best when he mentioned that vision without execution is hallucination. If you are not working toward achieving your dream culture, vision is just words on a whiteboard or on paper. It's all about having the right team on your side, all committed toward building a positive school culture through action.

Culture is not one person. It's everyone. Often in professional development workshops, the principal will ask me if they should invite their front office staff, custodians, paraprofessionals, school nutrition staff, and others to the Energy Bus workshop. Wholeheartedly, I say of course. I notice these teams are some of the most vocal during the workshops as they share their unique perspective on school improvement. Everyone in your building creates your culture.

However, school employees are not the only ones who can contribute to building a positive school culture. Schools need to be actively engaging with their parents. Numerous 2023 studies conducted by the US Department of Education found that parental involvement contributes to a more positive school climate, improved teacher morale, and stronger community support for schools. Schools with active parental engagement often experience reduced disciplinary issues and increased participation in extracurricular programs. Parents may hold the key to unlocking a thriving school culture, serving as the crucial link that often goes overlooked.

Connection Builders

Understand

There must be a key distinction between vision and core values as they relate to building a positive school culture. The vision answers "Where are we going?" while the core values answer "How do we behave as we work toward our vision?" For this question, gather into groups of four to six people and identify your school's core values. List a few words to describe the behaviors needed to work toward the vision.

____

____

____

____

Reflect

How can you ensure every staff member, from teachers to support staff, feels included in the culture-building process?

____

____

____

____

What opportunities exist for parents to actively participate in shaping the school's culture?

____

____

____

____

The Energy Bus for Schools Field Guide

Apply

What specific steps can your school take to increase parental engagement, particularly among families who are less involved?

____

____

____

____

What systems or processes are in place or need to be in place to ensure that the core values, identified above, are being lived and reinforced each day? How do others know these core values are real and define what the school stands for?

____

____

____

____

Team-Building Activities

1. One Word Cards

In the previous chapter, participants developed their One Words for their personal visions. The concept of One Word simplifies the vision creation and reinforcement process. Spirit Lake Elementary uses One Word cards that they strategically place around their campus and encourage faculty and students to look at as they enter various rooms or turn a corner in the hallway. These specific words will be referenced during classes and meetings as a reminder of what is important.

As a group, brainstorm a list of specific One Words that will be posted around campus. These can be your core value words or other words that should reflect the behaviors and mindset you want to see from the people inside your building. Utilize the school's art or graphics department to encourage students to create the words.

Build a Positive Culture

Use announcements and school social media to reinforce specific words throughout the year.

____

____

____

____

2. The Positive School Culture Team

All our Certified Energy Bus Schools have an Energy Bus Culture Team on campus. Since the school is involved in our Energy Bus for Schools Certified Program, they work with Energy Bus classroom activities, staff resources, coaching, and staff activities all school year. More information on the program can be found at www.EnergyBusForSchools .com or scanning the QR near the back of the field guide.

This Energy Bus Culture Team includes individuals from various departments on campus tasked with one goal: school culture. They are in charge of making sure the Energy Bus for Schools program is fully implemented in a creative and relevant way on campus.

For this activity, seek volunteers to be on a Positive School Culture Team. These individuals will help turn many of the ideas generated from using this field guide into reality. They will be the liaisons between the campus leadership team and the faculty/staff/students. Team members should be deeply invested in fostering a positive school culture. Establish the team, clearly define their roles, schedule regular meetings, and watch as their efforts transform the campus.

3. Develop a Positive Campus Plan

This is the first task of the Positive School Culture Team with the help of everyone on campus. Many schools that I have worked with over the last two decades have shared their simple ideas to build a positive campus culture. For example, some schools have teachers greet students at the door no matter the grade level. Other schools do emotional check-ins with students to see how everyone is feeling. This can be done anonymously with students writing on cards and turning them into a specific box at the beginning of class. Teachers can also have students put a specific laminated colored paper on their desk that coincides with a key of what emotion goes with each specific color.

Some schools use a loop system that keeps elementary classes together over multiple years to build stronger class bonds over the years. Middle and high schools use strong advisory systems where teachers act as advisors and mentors and meet with students regularly throughout their time on campus. Each system is a unique way to strengthen relationships.

Use this section to build your own campus plan with specific ideas and actions like the ones mentioned here. What new systems or processes could be added, and which existing ones on campus could be refined or improved? Be sure to brainstorm ideas that will work for your campus and identify an execution plan to communicate how it will be done and when it will start.

Added	Adjusted

Build a Positive Culture

4. Connection Circles

Ongoing professional development is a vital source of inspiration, knowledge, and strategies that can benefit educators throughout the year. Studies show that sustained and high-quality professional development can increase teacher effectiveness and retention. For example, a report from the Learning Policy Institute highlights that ongoing, collaborative learning aligned with teachers' daily responsibilities significantly impacts teaching strategies and student learning.

This is why the International School of Beijing has been intentional about sharing with faculty and staff the reason behind the importance of developing a positive and productive culture. They provide targeted meetings with all team leaders about tools that they can put in their teacher leadership tool box. This includes discussions regarding the research on positive relational energy, positive reframing, and joint accountability between administrators and staff for a solutions-based approach to challenges that exist.

For this activity, brainstorm the professional development topics your staff wants to learn more about during the school year. Give groups of four to six people time to discuss and then share all their answers on a flipchart paper in front of the room. You can take many of the ideas and put them on unique flipchart papers around the room. Give your staff time to walk around, view each professional development idea, and add comments or stars to their favorite ones as well as insights, sources, or ideas to teach it. In the end, pick 5–10 topics, assign key staff members to a team for each idea, and schedule the sessions throughout the year. The teaching team should be prepared to create a short, interactive lesson on each topic. Additionally, the school should consider inviting in-district or out-of-district speakers to present on the selected topics.

5. Culture Reflection Walk Activity

To facilitate a Culture Reflection Walk, first identify four to six key areas of school culture to reflect on, such as communication, teamwork, student relationships, and parental involvement. Set up stations around the room, each dedicated to one area, with materials like posters, flipchart paper, markers, and sticky notes for participants to visually and verbally contribute. Develop prompts that foster reflective, forward-thinking discussions, guiding staff to think critically about both strengths and areas for improvement (see suggestions at the end of this activity).

During execution, divide the staff into small groups of four to six people, rotating them through each station in timed intervals (e.g., five to seven minutes per station). At each station, group members will discuss the prompt, write down their insights, and highlight key themes or ideas left by previous groups. Participants should use provided sticky notes and place their answers on each flipchart paper hung on the wall. After rotating through all stations, the whole group will come back together to share insights, summarize recurring themes, and identify specific next steps to improve school culture.

Here are some examples of questions to use at different stations:

School Pride and Strengths

- What makes you most proud to be a part of this school?

- What recent accomplishments reflect the best of our school culture?

- Which traditions or practices bring the most joy to students and staff?

Opportunities for Growth

- What challenges do we face as a school community?

- What is one small change that could make a big difference for staff morale?

- What barriers exist to fostering better relationships with students and families?

Collaboration and Teamwork

- What does effective teamwork look like in our school?

- How can we support each other to create a more positive environment?

- What communication tools or strategies could help us collaborate better?

Student-Centered Culture

- How can we make students feel more valued and heard in our school?

- What activities or initiatives could better reflect the diverse needs of our students?

- What are we doing well in promoting student engagement, and where can we improve?

Build a Positive Culture

- What are we doing to engage parents effectively?

- How can we strengthen partnerships with community organizations?

- What events or initiatives could foster stronger school-community connections?

Case Study: Building a Resilient School Culture at Rocky Mount Elementary

Rocky Mount Elementary faced the challenge of fostering resilience among students and implemented a transformative process centered on a clear vision: creating a culture where every student develops the confidence to overcome obstacles, the resilience to face challenges, and the drive to pursue lifelong learning. This would define their school culture. Recognizing that resilience is a skill built through positive relationships, consistent support, and a growth-focused environment, the school developed a common language that unified how teachers responded to student struggles. This shared approach created a cohesive support system, making resilience-building an integral part of every classroom interaction.

By embedding this language into daily routines, school assemblies, and even the curriculum, students internalized the principles of positive thinking and perseverance. When challenges arose, students learned to view setbacks not as failures but as valuable learning opportunities. Teachers reinforced this mindset by using consistent strategies and language, promoting a culture of shared responsibility for personal growth. Over time, resilience became more than a concept, as it evolved into a defining feature of Rocky Mount's identity, empowering students to thrive both academically and personally.

Principal Matt Dunbar and staff celebrate being a Certified Energy Bus School.

Best Practices and Main Takeaways

- **Vision must be paired with action**
  - A school's vision and mission create identity, but without implementation, it's just words.
  - Schools must take actionable steps involving all staff members to bring the vision and mission to life through consistent behavior aligned with core values.

- **Include all staff and stakeholders**
  - Building a positive culture requires contributions from all school employees, including teachers, administrators, support staff, and even parents.
  - Everyone plays a role, offering diverse perspectives and strengthening the school's collective mission.

- **Parental engagement is a key factor**
  - Active parental involvement leads to a more supportive school environment.
  - It improves teacher morale, boosts student success, and fosters strong school-community relationships.
  - Schools should create intentional opportunities for parents to participate.

- **Support structured team and leadership development**
  - Schools benefit from establishing dedicated culture teams, such as the Positive School Culture Team.
  - These teams sustain schoolwide initiatives and ensure continuous improvement.
  - Regular professional development and team-building activities help maintain momentum and strengthen staff collaboration.

- **Provide for reflection and continuous improvement**
  - Schools must regularly evaluate their culture through reflection walks, brainstorming sessions, and feedback exercises.
  - This reflective process ensures the school continually evolves while reinforcing its core values and collective vision.

Personal Reflection

How could the new knowledge, skills, and strategies from this section impact your campus and your role?

Build a Positive Culture

Chapter 3

Fuel Your Ride with Positive Energy

Every school feels the impact of energy, whether it is positive or negative. It shapes the atmosphere, influences relationships, and drives results. The quote "Where the focus goes, the energy flows" reminds us that what we choose to emphasize directly affects the culture we create. This section builds on the foundation of the previous two by equipping you with uplifting strategies and intentional actions that fuel lasting positivity, keep momentum strong, and help your school community thrive all year long.

Extensive research demonstrates the tangible benefits of positive thinking and optimism for both mental and physical health. For instance, a study by the Mayo Clinic indicates that positive thinking is a key component of effective stress management, which is associated with numerous health benefits.

In schools, fostering a positive environment can enhance performance. Studies have shown that when high-performing teams maintain a higher ratio of positive to negative interactions it correlates with improved outcomes.

As I visited many campuses over the years, it was obvious which schools were focused on fueling everyone's ride with positive energy. As you read in the previous section's case study, Rocky Mount Elementary has been focused on creating the most engaged and positive campus they can create possible. They are intentional in building systems that allow positive energy to fuel the ride for both students and staff. Feeding the positive and sharing encouragement and motivation have become part of their daily practice at Rocky Mount.

People generally want to feel happy, valued, and engaged in their work. If school leaders can create an atmosphere that allows staff to feel all three at a high level, there is a greater chance of keeping people long term and encouraging them to engage more in their work. Anyone in education knows how much effort and time it takes to create a collaborative and positive school community. It involves both parents and staff coming together to volunteer their time in unique ways. When a community is truly engaged, its members become more motivated and driven to put in the effort needed to achieve lasting, sustainable results.

This section is about keeping energy high during the entire school year. Everyone is excited and anxious at the beginning, but November, February, and April matter just as much. Sustaining positive energy throughout the school year ensures that every month counts, transforming temporary excitement into lasting momentum and meaningful success.

Connection Builders

Understand

What does "fueling your ride with positive energy" mean to you personally?

____

____

____

____

How do your thoughts and actions impact the energy you bring to school each day?

____

____

____

____

____

____

The Energy Bus for Schools Field Guide

Think of a time when your positive attitude helped you overcome a challenging situation. What did you learn from that experience?

____

____

____

____

____

Think about current practices at the school related to addressing faculty and staff well-being and mental health. If you had to assign a number from 1 to 10, with 10 being the highest, how would you rank current practices and why?

____

____

____

____

____

How do you generally feel about coming to school each day? Elaborate on your response and share with others.

____

____

____

____

____

Apply

What specific actions can you take daily to fuel yourself with positive energy before coming to school? How can this impact your students and colleagues?

____

____

____

____

How can your team create a culture where positive energy is consistently encouraged and supported, even during challenging times?

____

____

____

____

What classroom routines or activities can you implement to help students recognize and build positive energy throughout the day?

____

____

____

____

Team-Building Activities

1. "This Is Why" Wall

The "This Is Why" Wall activity helps staff reconnect with their passion for teaching and education by reflecting on meaningful career moments and sharing them with colleagues. Set up a visually appealing display in a high-traffic area like the staff lounge or

The Energy Bus for Schools Field Guide

front office, using bulletin board paper, posters, or precut cards. Include prompts such as "Why did you become a teacher?" or "What teaching moment made you smile recently?" or "What do you like most about your role?" Staff can write responses anonymously or include their names, contributing to a supportive and motivational school environment.

To maintain engagement, refresh the wall monthly or spotlight select stories during staff meetings. Consider creating a digital version through platforms like Padlet or Google Jamboard. Extend the activity by involving students with a companion wall expressing their appreciation for teachers and other staff members. Use the wall for special events like Teacher Appreciation Week or as a reflective tool during professional development sessions. This ongoing project fosters a culture of positivity, purpose, and shared inspiration throughout the school year.

2. Positivity Post-it Wall and Digital Platforms

The Positivity Post-it Wall is a simple yet impactful activity designed to boost staff morale and build a supportive school culture. Set up a board in a central staff area labeled "Fuel Your Ride with Positivity." Provide colorful Post-it notes and encourage staff to write short, uplifting messages recognizing their colleagues' contributions (e.g., "Thank you for helping me with my lesson plan!"). Regularly read a few notes aloud during team meetings to spread positivity, promote appreciation, and reinforce a culture of gratitude and teamwork.

Schools can foster a culture of positivity through regular shoutouts shared via digital platforms. At Spirit Lake Elementary, teachers use a Google Form to submit shoutouts, which are read during daily announcements, spreading positivity among students and staff while reinforcing Energy Bus principles. Similarly, at the International School of Beijing, faculty submit Gratitude Shoutouts through a Microsoft Form, which is published weekly in the staff bulletin, ensuring consistent recognition and a supportive school environment.

Clubs can be for more than students. At Coshocton High School in Ohio, they promote staff wellness and connection by organizing Coffee Club Fridays, where cafeteria staff brew a large pot of coffee and staff bring seasonal coffee creamers. Music adds to the cheerful atmosphere.

Additionally, some staff participate in a walking club before school, using indoor tracks or hallways during colder months and enjoying the outdoor track on warmer days. These activities foster camaraderie, boost morale, and encourage healthy habits among staff. While they are all voluntary, Coshocton High School reports consistently high attendance at both clubs throughout the year.

Brainstorm similar clubs that can work on your campus. What would be the main focus and activity, and who would organize it? How would it be promoted to the adult school community?

____

____

____

____

____

____

____

____

____

____

____

____

4. Student Recognition

At Dayton High School, students are honored as "Drivers of the Month" for consistently demonstrating the core principles of the Energy Bus. This recognition celebrates those who lead with positivity, take ownership of their attitude, and help create a supportive, energized school culture by living out specific Energy Bus rules. Every teacher selects a student who best embodies the month's featured Energy Bus rule, significantly expanding recognition from just 8 students per month to over 20. Honorees receive a donut, have their picture taken holding a sign with the corresponding Energy Bus rule, and see their laminated photo displayed above their teacher's classroom door, reinforcing positive behavior throughout the school.

Similarly, Franklin Elementary School shifted from a traditional "Star Student" model to "Drivers of the Week," allowing all students to share their passions and be celebrated by the year's end. The school also introduced the "Chief Energy Officer" award, recognizing students who consistently live out Energy Bus principles. These initiatives encourage staff and students to bring positive energy daily while fostering a culture of recognition, inclusion, and community.

Analyze your school's current student recognition program. Is there anything that needs to be changed, and how can it be improved to incorporate an Energy Bus theme?

Fuel Your Ride with Positive Energy

5. Innovative Professional Development

The Energy Bus for Schools book mentioned (on page 52) a professional development (PD) activity called "Carver at Night" by the Anne Arundel School District in Maryland. The experience includes dinner and a variety of fun and innovative sessions staff members can choose from, including yoga, massage, and professional learning. There is always a waiting list to attend this annual PD event.

This professional development experience effectively fuels staff motivation and engagement. It's a unique approach that makes employees feel valued and supported, reinforcing that their district genuinely cares about their growth and well-being. The district's commitment to creating a meaningful and memorable experience is evident through their thoughtful planning and dedication.

For this exercise gather into groups of four to six people, and spend time planning a similar PD experience for the school. Get creative in your approach and design a session that will engage all who attend while making it fun, interactive, and informative. There must be some learning components built into the experience. Have fun and go beyond the boundaries of traditional PD!

The Energy Bus for Schools Field Guide

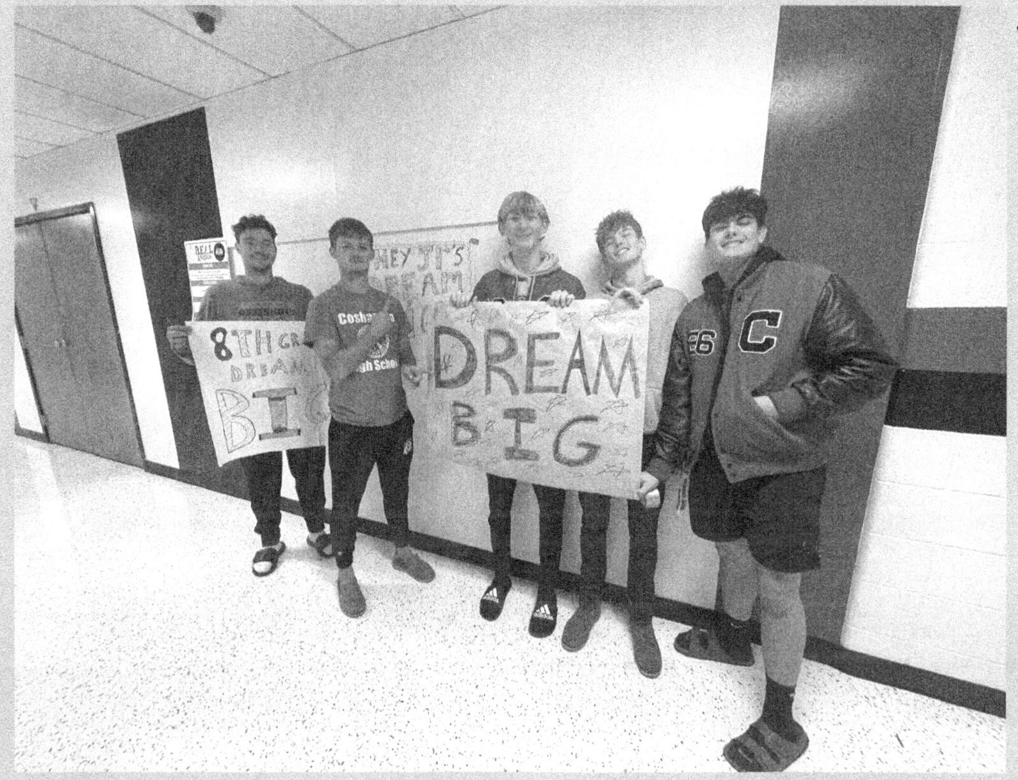

Coshocton High School has embraced *The Energy Bus* principle of "Fuel Your Ride with Positive Energy" by fostering a culture of collaboration, encouragement, and shared responsibility. Each morning, grade-level teams and departments gather for collaboration meetings where they share ideas and troubleshoot challenges. To uplift team morale, administrators, counselors, and Energy Bus program leaders join meetings when groups seem discouraged, and provide fresh perspectives and support. This collaborative spirit energizes staff and reinforces a shared commitment to positivity. Additionally, the school has adopted the "No Complaining Rule"

(continued)

during meetings, requiring staff to suggest three potential solutions when presenting concerns. This practice encourages proactive problem-solving and helps maintain a constructive team environment.

The school's culture of positivity extends beyond meetings into daily routines and
community-building traditions. Faculty members participate in a Secret Santa or Secret
Pal activity, guided by personalized "What Fuels Their Ride" forms listing favorite
items and treats. This thoughtful exchange strengthens connections and boosts staff
morale. Daily announcements featuring Energy Bus quotes or themes remind students and staff of their shared values, reinforcing a positive culture throughout the
campus. By combining structured collaboration, meaningful recognition, and positive reinforcement, Coshocton High School continuously fuels its community with
positive energy, ensuring everyone stays energized and focused on success.

 **Best Practices and Main Takeaways**

- **Positive energy drives school success**

  - Positive energy impacts mental and physical well-being, reducing stress and improving performance.

  - Schools that prioritize positive interactions see better academic and behavioral outcomes.

- **Intentional culture building is key**

  - Establishing systems that encourage encouragement and collaboration sustains positive energy.

  - Schools like Rocky Mount Elementary create intentional programs that support both students and staff daily.

- **Community engagement strengthens positivity**

  - Staff and parents working together enhance motivation and foster a supportive environment.

  - Volunteer-driven events and collaborative projects build lasting school-community bonds.

- **Consistent recognition reinforces values**

  - Recognizing students and staff for living out positive principles keeps the school's values visible.

  - Programs like "Drivers of the Month" and teacher shoutouts reinforce a culture of appreciation and inclusion.

- **Sustain effort throughout the year**

  - It's not just about starting strong because schools must maintain positive energy through every season.

  - Creative team-building, recognition programs, and professional development events help sustain enthusiasm all year long.

Fuel Your Ride with Positive Energy

Personal Reflection

How could the new knowledge, skills, and strategies from this section impact your campus and your role?

The Energy Bus for Schools Field Guide

Chapter 4

Love Your Passengers

A school will only be successful if they work together as a team to make the vision into reality. Despite the challenges of today's education system, educators have to learn to work together and put students first. Everyone has different backgrounds, perspectives, and ideas, but the end goal is always to turn the school into a destination location. A place where people line up to work there, families want to move to the area for the schools, and the energy is off the charts. It starts at the mindset level when it comes to people and relationships and it is very simple: Relational maintenance and improvement are a choice.

The school days are long and tiring and sometimes the silence is comforting in between busy classrooms and hallways. However, too much isolation and silence from colleagues will eventually cause division. Educators need to lean into building the relationships around them. It's time to invite others on the bus and love your passengers.

But love does not stop at the staff level. It must permeate all throughout campus, so it becomes something that people just think, feel, and live. Love must be an action on campus that unites and binds everyone together into a community and a campus family. Love makes students feel like they belong on campus. They don't feel like a number. They feel safe, heard, validated, understood, and appreciated.

The previous section highlighted Coshocton High School, a Certified Energy Bus School in Ohio, and how they fuel the ride of everyone on campus. Their staff and students put love into action every day and have many stories to tell. One particularly moving story came from a seventh-grade student who shared an experience that left a lasting impression. While walking to school on a rainy morning, the student was unexpectedly offered a ride by a senior girl who had never met her before. Despite being late herself, the senior went out of her way to help. The younger student described the moment as "one of the nicest things anyone has ever done for her" and emphasized how it exemplified the school's value of "truly loving all their passengers." This simple yet powerful act of kindness illustrates how fostering a culture of care can strengthen community bonds and inspire others to lead with empathy and generosity.

Connection Builders

Reflect

Think about a time when someone's kindness or support had a significant impact on your life. How did it influence your perspective or actions toward others?

____

____

____

____

____

Love is supposed to bring people together. Reflect on your current feelings toward loving others who are different from you, have different ideas, or are not in your immediate circle.

____

____

____

____

____

The Energy Bus for Schools Field Guide

Understand

Why is building positive relationships on campus essential for both staff and students? How does a supportive environment impact learning and school culture?

How can embracing diverse perspectives among staff members contribute to a stronger, more connected school community?

Love Your Passengers

Apply

It's time to put love into action. Using the chart below, identify specific things you can do to love your passengers. If in a group, ask various participants to share their responses and celebrate the answers.

Ways to Love Your Passengers	Family	Staff Members (Colleagues)	Students	Parents
Make time for them	_______	_______	_______	_______
	_______	_______	_______	_______
	_______	_______	_______	_______
	_______	_______	_______	_______
	_______	_______	_______	_______
	_______	_______	_______	_______
Listen to them	_______	_______	_______	_______
	_______	_______	_______	_______
	_______	_______	_______	_______
	_______	_______	_______	_______
	_______	_______	_______	_______
	_______	_______	_______	_______
Recognize them	_______	_______	_______	_______
	_______	_______	_______	_______
	_______	_______	_______	_______
	_______	_______	_______	_______
	_______	_______	_______	_______
	_______	_______	_______	_______

Ways to Love Your Passengers	Family	Staff Members (Colleagues)	Students	Parents
Serve them	_________	_________	_________	_________
	_________	_________	_________	_________
	_________	_________	_________	_________
	_________	_________	_________	_________
	_________	_________	_________	_________
	_________	_________	_________	_________
Bring out the best in them	_________	_________	_________	_________
	_________	_________	_________	_________
	_________	_________	_________	_________
	_________	_________	_________	_________
	_________	_________	_________	_________
	_________	_________	_________	_________

Team-Building Activities

1. Love Through Appreciation

To cultivate a culture of appreciation and recognition, schools can implement simple yet meaningful practices that celebrate both staff and students. One idea from Spirit Lake Elementary is to use yellow bus-shaped cards to write personalized notes highlighting staff members' positive contributions. Attaching a small treat adds a thoughtful touch. It's essential to include all staff members, from teachers to support personnel, ensuring everyone feels valued. Additionally, Franklin Elementary staff send home "Good News" postcards recognizing students' accomplishments, positive behavior, or acts of kindness. These notes not only celebrate students but also strengthen the home-school connection by sharing uplifting updates with families.

Encouraging mutual appreciation among staff can be achieved through a "Pay It Forward" system, where recognized staff members pass along blank cards to acknowledge others. Schools like Coshocton High School engage students by allowing them to nominate staff members for "Staff of the Month" and share heartfelt reasons for their selections. These nominations can be read aloud during assemblies and posted on recognition boards or social media. By embedding these intentional practices into the school culture, appreciation becomes a regular, meaningful experience that deepens connections and fosters a positive, supportive environment.

Reflect on the above activities and brainstorm how they might work on your campus. Write your thoughts down, then share your ideas with the whole group and select a few ideas to implement in your school or department.

---

2. 2 × 10 Relationship-Building Strategy

The "2 × 10 Relationship Builder Challenge" encourages educators to strengthen student relationships by committing to the 2 × 10 method: having two-minute, non-academic conversations with a selected student for 10 consecutive school days. Educators can pair up to discuss challenges they face in building student connections and brainstorm conversation starters. Each participant chooses one student to focus on, identifies potential discussion topics, and plans when and where the daily check-ins will happen.

To promote accountability and encouragement, schools can create a visual "Commitment Wall" where staff post anonymous notes like "I'm committed to meaningful conversations." After two weeks, educators reconvene to reflect on progress, sharing observed improvements in student behavior or engagement. This challenge fosters collaboration among staff while creating a more supportive, trusting school environment built on strong student-teacher relationships.

Within just five months of implementing the initiative at a Philadelphia middle school, the school is already seeing notable improvements. For example, the school reported positive changes in the district's quarterly student well-being survey. The results showed that 96% of students indicated having positive relationships with their teachers, reflecting a 6.6% increase from the previous quarter. Additionally, there was a 7.37% rise in students expressing positive views about all their interpersonal relationships at school.

How would this strategy work on campus? What would be your expected results? Brainstorm a plan to make this a reality or come up with something similar.

____

____

____

____

____

3. Acts of Kindness

One notable example of kindness and love in action is Washington Elementary's "Kindness Challenge," where the school aimed to document 5,000 random acts of kindness within 15 days. This initiative not only met its goal but also transformed the school's culture, encouraging students to engage in compassionate behaviors and recognize the impact of their actions on others.

To replicate Washington Elementary's Kindness Challenge, schools can organize a Kindness Countdown Challenge lasting two weeks. The school sets a collective goal, such as documenting 5,000 random acts of kindness, and tracks progress on a large "Kindness Wall" in a central hallway. The challenge kicks off with an assembly or video announcement explaining the importance of kindness and how small acts can create a positive school culture. Each day, the school shares kindness tips or quotes during morning announcements, and students participate by performing and logging acts of kindness using cards or a digital platform. Teachers can hold quick classroom reflections at the end of the day, encouraging students to share their experiences and recognize others' efforts.

To build staff engagement, schools can run a parallel Staff Kindness Challenge with a smaller but equally meaningful target. Staff can give and receive Kindness Shoutouts during meetings or in newsletters, fostering a supportive environment. At the end of the challenge, the school can host a Kindness Assembly to celebrate, highlight meaningful stories, and recognize exceptional acts of kindness. This initiative can also be shared on social media, reinforcing a culture of compassion while connecting the school community through positive actions.

In groups of four to six, discuss how engaging an activity like this would work for your campus. Consider how it could be planned and implemented effectively, and explore the potential impact it could have on your school community.

4. Connection Card Bingo

Take time to build meaningful relationships by connecting with others whose names can be written in the spaces below to complete a Bingo. After a few rounds, invite participants to share interesting stories related to one of the prompts with the entire group or within smaller groups of four to six people.

Find someone who has taught at this school for over 5 years	Find someone who loves the same hobby as you	Find someone who was born in the same month as you	Find someone who speaks more than one language	Find someone who has run a marathon or a race
Find someone who has visited another continent	Find someone who has a pet other than a dog or cat	Find someone who plays a musical instrument	Find someone who enjoys cooking or baking	Find someone who has read more than 5 books this year
Find someone who loves outdoor activities	Find someone who has worked in education for over 10 years	FREE SPACE	Find someone who has attended a live concert this year	Find someone who volunteers in their community
Find someone who enjoys gardening	Find someone who has a hidden talent	Find someone who has completed a DIY project recently	Find someone who has participated in a sports team	Find someone who is an early riser
Find someone who loves to watch movies or TV shows	Find someone who prefers coffee over tea	Find someone who has tried a new hobby recently	Find someone who has been to a national park	Find someone who enjoys art or crafts

5. Safe Spaces

Safe Spaces is a team-building exercise designed to strengthen relationships by fostering empathy and understanding among school staff. Participants form a large circle while a facilitator reads prompts encouraging individuals to step into the circle if the statement applies to them. Each circle should consist of no more than 20–30 participants, so schools may want to consider creating multiple circles. Prompts could include "Step into the circle if you've ever helped a colleague through a tough day," "Step in if you've had a student make your day brighter," or "Step in if you've ever made a positive phone call home." After each prompt, those who stepped into the circle return to their spots, and the facilitator invites a few volunteers to share personal stories connected to the prompt. This sharing creates a safe space where educators can reflect, connect, and celebrate meaningful experiences.

This activity is impactful because it highlights shared experiences, fostering a sense of belonging and mutual support. Seeing colleagues step forward reminds participants that they are not alone in their challenges or triumphs. The shared stories encourage vulnerability and inspire deeper conversations beyond the activity. Safe Spaces can be adapted for various team-building events throughout the school year to maintain a supportive, collaborative school culture.

Sample Prompts

Professional Support and Teamwork

Step into the circle if you've ever …

covered for a colleague in an emergency.

shared teaching materials or lesson plans with a teammate.

mentored a new staff member or been mentored yourself.

asked a colleague for help and felt supported.

worked late or come in early to support your team.

celebrated a colleague's personal or professional achievement.

Student Relationships and Success

Step into the circle if you've ever ...

seen a student overcome a major challenge in your class.

written a positive note to a student or parent.

felt emotional due to a student's success.

been inspired by a student's resilience or determination.

been visited by a former student after moving on.

supported a student outside of academics (socially or emotionally).

School and Community Impact

Step into the circle if you've ever ...

volunteered at a school event or fundraiser.

led or helped with a school initiative.

represented your school at a community event.

written a grant or secured funding for your school.

supported a community service project involving students.

organized or participated in a school spirit event.

Personal and Emotional Connection

Step into the circle if you've ever ...

felt inspired by your work, despite challenges.

received a student thank-you note that meant a lot to you.

been surprised by a colleague's kind gesture.

reflected on how much your work matters.

felt truly appreciated by someone at school.

made a lasting friendship with a colleague.

Love Your Passengers

To create a culture of continuous recognition and love, Greensboro Academy developed a comprehensive system focused on intentional scheduling, team-building events, and consistent acknowledgment of positive behavior. A detailed culture calendar includes fun events like themed dress days, cookie swaps, taco bars, and ice cream socials. Staff earn "bus tickets" for participating, entering them into prize drawings, making recognition fun and engaging.

Administrators use an internal recognition system to celebrate staff when they are seen doing something positive. They award bus tickets and select "Bus Drivers of the Week," who are announced during school assemblies. Students earn stars through a schoolwide Energy Bus Star Chart, working toward classroom rewards. Monthly moral focus assemblies highlight students who earn bus tickets, while buddy classrooms collaborate on shared learning activities. Staff birthdays are celebrated with monthly treats and recognition on the school's front sign. This consistent, genuine approach ensures that appreciation remains an integral part of the school culture year-round. Appreciation and love go together to create a school culture where everyone feels valued.

When a student with a history of significant disciplinary issues transferred to Franklin Elementary School, he arrived with the expectation of being judged negatively. His past experiences left him guarded and disconnected, assuming he would be labeled as a "problem student." However, the staff took a different approach, focusing on understanding his unique strengths. Through conversations, they discovered his deep love and protective nature toward his younger cousins, who were also enrolled at the school.

(continued)

Recognizing this as a powerful leadership quality, the staff created opportunities for him to serve as a student leader, helping younger students and acting as a role model. This responsibility allowed him to see himself in a new, positive light. As he embraced these roles, he began extending the care he felt for his cousins to other students, fostering stronger connections and developing a sense of belonging.

This shift transformed not only his behavior but also his confidence and self-worth. He no longer saw himself as a troubled student but rather as someone capable of making a meaningful impact. Through intentional support, trust, and encouragement, he flourished within a compassionate school environment where his strengths were recognized and nurtured. He felt loved by a staff that did not just label him and move on. They recognized his strengths and leveraged them to help others.

Case Study: Love Across the Generations

Clarke Prep School in Alabama exemplifies what it means to be a Certified Energy Bus School. Nestled in a close-knit, small-town community where everyone knows each other, this pre-K–12 school fosters a supportive environment where many students spend up to 14 years on campus. Their commitment to engaging every part of their school community is evident through creative events and initiatives.

Recently, Clarke Prep hosted a heartwarming "Grandparents Day" on campus, featuring food, fun, and meaningful activities. As part of their Energy Bus journey, they invited grandparents to participate in a weekly Energy Bus activity alongside students. The experience was so impactful that many grandparents described it as one of their best days ever.

While schools often focus on students, staff, and parents, including the grandparents creates a deeper, more connected community. After all, getting everyone "on the bus" truly means everyone. Consider opening your school's doors to all who are connected to your campus to highlight your unique culture and demonstrate that your school is a place of hope, love, and joy.

Best Practices and Main Takeaways

- **Relationships are a choice**
  - Building a positive school culture starts with choosing to form meaningful relationships with colleagues, students, and families.
  - Fostering connections prevents isolation and division among staff and creates a collaborative environment.

- **Love must be an action**
  - Love should be more than a concept. It should be demonstrated through daily actions, showing kindness, support, and understanding across the entire school community.
  - Acts of kindness, recognition, and service create a sense of belonging and safety for students and staff.

- **Staff and student recognition strengthens community**
  - Regular recognition programs like "Staff of the Month" or "Drivers of the Week" motivate staff and students to embody positive values.
  - Celebrating achievements publicly reinforces a culture of appreciation and shared purpose.

- **Act intentionally to create a supportive environment**
  - Activities like the "Kindness Challenge," personalized notes, and teacher-student relationship programs strengthen the school's emotional climate.
  - Structured team-building events like Connection Card Bingo or Safe Spaces promote empathy and understanding.

- **Engage families and the wider community**
  - Schools can deepen bonds by including families in events like Grandparents Day or student-centered leadership roles.
  - Creating opportunities for multigenerational involvement reinforces a supportive, inclusive school culture.

Personal Reflection

How could the new knowledge, skills, and strategies from this section impact your campus and your role?

Chapter 5

Transform Negativity

The human heart produces the strongest electromagnetic field in the body. Research from the HeartMath Institute shows that this magnetic field can be measured up to three feet away. What's fascinating is that this field changes depending on our emotions. Positive feelings like love and gratitude create a more balanced, stable heart rhythm, which can both improve personal well-being and influence the people around us in positive ways. Negativity affects us and others in negative ways.

Some scientists suggest that the brain might also act like an antenna, connecting to a larger universal field. Known as the "quantum brain" theory, this idea is still being explored but is based on the brain's natural ability to detect and respond to electromagnetic signals. While this theory is theoretical, it opens up interesting possibilities about how humans process emotions, thoughts, and even connections with others.

Emotions are hard to hide on a school campus. We're all human, and it's natural to experience emotional reactions and occasional conflicts. However, these challenges shouldn't deter us from building positive school environments. As the research suggests above, we can sense and feel people's emotional energy. By implementing and reinforcing strategies to transform negativity, schools can stay aligned with their visions of positivity, unity, and collaboration, which are essential values for preparing the next generation for success.

Rocky Mount Elementary exemplifies this approach by focusing on consistently bringing staff and students back to their shared vision of a positive school. They've learned how to navigate negativity in a productive way, ensuring that their school culture remains strong and supportive. With intentional practices, schools can overcome challenges while fostering a positive, collaborative atmosphere.

You cannot avoid negativity in school, but it is possible to understand it better and the root causes behind it.

Connection Builders

Reflect

Negativity exists in some form in all schools. The more you talk about it and identify it, the more you can recognize it occurring around you or because of you. Without being too obvious or identifying specific people, write, reflect, and share what negativity can look like on campus. Focus on behaviors and don't include names, job titles, or other descriptive details about the person.

____

____

____

____

Understand

How does the concept of the heart's electromagnetic field help explain how positive and negative emotions can impact those around us? Do you believe what the research suggests? Why or why not?

____

____

____

____

Why is it important to recognize how our emotions affect both ourselves and others on campus? How can this self-awareness shape school culture?

____

____

____

____

The Energy Bus for Schools Field Guide

Apply

What strategies can you personally apply to manage your emotional energy on difficult days? How can these strategies be taught to students?

What specific steps could your team take to address and reduce negativity on campus while promoting collaboration and unity?

Think of a time when your school successfully transformed a negative situation into a positive outcome. What intentional actions were taken, and how could similar strategies be applied in the future?

Transform Negativity

Team-Building Activities

1. Reframe and Respond

In this activity, educators work together to practice reframing negative situations into opportunities for growth. Divide participants into groups of four to six people and provide each group with real or hypothetical school-based scenarios involving challenging behavior, such as a student being disruptive in class or a staff conflict during a meeting. Each group discusses the situation, identifies potential root causes, and brainstorms supportive, growth-oriented responses that address the underlying issues. Afterward, groups share their strategies with the larger team, focusing on how reframing the challenge led to more constructive solutions.

As a bonus, staff members can role-play various experiences and reflect on tone, phrasing, and responses. This activity promotes collaboration, problem-solving, and the adoption of a positive, solutions-focused mindset across the school community.

School Scenario	Cause of Issues	Appropriate Response and Resolution
1.		
2.		
3.		
4.		
5.		

The Energy Bus for Schools Field Guide

2. STAR 3

In *The Energy Bus for Schools* book (pages 112–113), we share the STAR 3 Model, from Jon Gordon's book *Difficult Conversations Don't Have to Be Difficult*, that is used to handle difficult conversations and teach people strategies to navigate negativity.

STAR 3 in Review

S—Small ego. Big mission. We>Me.

T—Truth. Tell the truth in love to get better together.

A—Assume positive intent. Do not take it personally. Manage emotional energy. No personal attacks.

R1—Relationships matter most.

R2—Respect your team and the process. Truth told in love develops respect, and respect values truth.

R3—Rules of engagement. Create specific rules of engagement for your team to have difficult conversations in a positive way.

To begin the activity, divide participants into six teams of four to six people and assign each team one letter from the STAR 3 Model (S, T, A, R1, R2, or R3). Each team is responsible for understanding and exploring their assigned letter in depth.

Teams define their letter, and discuss how it applies to school culture, personal relationships, and everyday interactions on campus. This encourages meaningful reflection on how the principles of STAR 3 can be applied in real-life situations.

Next, teams brainstorm actionable strategies based on their assigned letter. These strategies should focus on improving communication, managing negativity, and fostering positive relationships. The goal is to develop practical solutions that can be implemented within the school environment.

Afterward, each team presents their letter, definition, and proposed strategies to the larger group. The facilitator leads a reflective discussion on how these strategies can strengthen trust, respect, and collaboration within the school community. This activity promotes teamwork, shared responsibility, and a commitment to building a

Transform Negativity

positive culture through honest and respectful communication. The school may want to consider providing flipchart paper and markers to each group so they can share their responses in a visual manner.

3. Create and Commit to a "No Complaining Rule"

This activity helps educators develop and implement their own No Complaining Rule based on Jon Gordon's book *The No Complaining Rule: Positive Ways to Deal with Negativity at Work,* which encourages a culture focused on solutions rather than problems. Begin by explaining the rule: Avoid mindless complaining to others and bring concerns to the right person with one or more possible solutions. Discuss how shifting from negativity to problem-solving can create a more positive school environment.

Divide educators into small teams of four to six people and ask them to brainstorm common school-related complaints, such as workload or communication issues. Each group selects two complaints and reframes them by creating actionable solutions. This step encourages creative thinking, collaboration, and a positive mindset.

Next, teams design a personalized No Complaining Rule Commitment Poster for their school, including guiding principles and solution-based practices. Finally, they present their ideas to the larger group. This will inspire and strengthen everyone's shared commitment to creating a supportive, solutions-focused school culture where positivity and progress thrive.

4. Unmet Needs

In *The Energy Bus for Schools* book (pages 104–107), we discuss unmet needs and how they can lead to negativity and conflict. According to the textbook *Interpersonal Conflict* (Hocker, Wilmot, and Berry; McGraw Hill, 2021), incompatible goals between two people are often a driving force behind conflict, too. Usually, someone or something is preventing us from achieving a goal related to one of our basic needs: attachment, acceptance, positive regard, autonomy, and competence. Here is a brief review of each one:

1. **Attachment:** Attachment is the need for emotional connection and meaningful relationships with others. When unmet, individuals may feel isolated, unsupported, or disconnected, impacting their ability to trust and engage with others.

2. **Acceptance:** Acceptance involves feeling valued and included by others, regardless of differences or imperfections. When this need is unmet, individuals may experience feelings of rejection, loneliness, or inadequacy.

3. **Positive Regard:** Positive regard refers to being seen and treated with respect, kindness, and unconditional care. Without it, individuals may struggle with low self-esteem and feel unworthy or undervalued in personal or professional relationships.

4. **Autonomy:** Autonomy is the need to have control over one's actions, choices, and direction in life. When autonomy is restricted, individuals may feel powerless, restricted, or overly dependent on others, leading to frustration and decreased motivation.

5. **Competence:** Competence is the need to feel capable, effective, and successful in completing tasks and achieving goals. If this need goes unmet, individuals may doubt their abilities, experience low self-confidence, and struggle with motivation or performance.

Using the above information, rank your most important needs 1 through 5, with 1 being the biggest need. Simply write your number next to the need. In the large group, have a facilitator ask people to raise their hand for who selected each need as their top answer. Use the following prompts to guide meaningful discussions with your staff, either as a whole group or in smaller breakout groups. Each group should be given 3 to 5 minutes to discuss each prompt. After each round, the facilitator should invite a few groups to share their top takeaways or most impactful responses with the larger group.

- **Self-Reflection and Sharing:** Reflect on a time when one of these needs (attachment, acceptance, positive regard, autonomy, or competence) went unmet in your personal or professional life. How did it affect your behavior or relationships? What helped you overcome the challenge?

- **School Environment and Culture:** How can unmet needs contribute to negativity or conflict in a school environment among staff or students? What specific strategies could your school implement to address these needs and create a more supportive culture?

- **Conflict Resolution and Growth:** Think about a conflict you've experienced at work or school. Looking back, which unmet need might have been driving the conflict? How could recognizing that need have helped you respond differently or find a positive resolution?

Case Study: Embracing a Solutions-Focused Approach at the International School of Beijing

At the International School of Beijing, our first international Certified Energy Bus School, they have cultivated an environment where discussions around challenges and collaboration thrive. By recognizing the diverse experiences of individuals in the presence of challenges, the leadership team has fostered meaningful conversations around energy and collaboration. The leadership team expanded the No Complaining Rule using a social–emotional learning (SEL) perspective, transforming how staff approach challenges during collaborative planning meetings. This shift has promoted a shared sense of responsibility for maintaining both productivity and positivity in the school's work culture.

To empower staff in navigating challenges, the leadership team introduced a structured, empathetic approach. Individuals were guided to identify and name the challenge while acknowledging the associated emotions, recognizing that experiencing difficulties is both normal and healthy. Staff were encouraged to see challenges as opportunities by brainstorming one or two potential solutions. If a clear solution wasn't immediately available, seeking assistance was normalized as a constructive and valuable response. This process reframed problems as opportunities for growth, fostering a culture of support, improvement, and collaborative problem-solving throughout the school community.

The Energy Bus for Schools Field Guide

Transform Negativity

Case Study: Turning Challenges into Change: Transforming Negativity at Cimarron Public School

Understanding negativity, anxiety, and fear begins with uncovering their root causes. During a student assembly at Cimarron Public School in Oklahoma, I took a different approach. Rather than delivering a traditional keynote speech, I set up interactive flipchart stations around the gym, each with a thought-provoking prompt. Students wrote anonymous responses on Post-it notes and placed them on the corresponding charts. Prompts ranged from reflections on Energy Bus rules to deeper questions like "What are your biggest challenges or struggles?" This activity created a safe space for honest sharing.

As I reviewed the responses, a stark reality emerged: many students faced overwhelming challenges, including addiction, loneliness, bullying, family loss, and financial struggles. Moved by these insights, I brought the flipcharts into the faculty's professional development session later that day for their teachers to view. Seeing students' words humanized their struggles, prompting the staff to commit to rolling out the Energy Bus principles with renewed focus on relationships and mental health. They also pledged to expand campus resources, offering students additional support. Cimarron Public School is now on a transformative journey, determined to replace negativity with empowerment and create a stronger, more compassionate school environment.

Best Practices and Main Takeaways

- **Emotions impact school culture**

  - The heart's electromagnetic field influences emotions, affecting both the individual and those around them.

  - Positive emotions like love and gratitude create balanced, stable energy that can uplift the school environment, while negative emotions can create tension and conflict.

- **Understand the root causes of negativity**

  - Recognizing the root causes of negativity helps in managing it effectively.

  - Common unmet needs like attachment, acceptance, autonomy, and competence can drive negative behaviors in schools if left unaddressed.

- **Transform negativity into growth opportunities**

  - Schools can adopt strategies like reframing negative situations into learning moments.

  - Practices such as the No Complaining Rule encourage solution-based thinking, reducing conflict and fostering collaboration.

- **Know the power of intentional actions**

  - Activities like team-building exercises, empathy-based discussions, and creating schoolwide behavioral norms help transform school culture.

  - Structured systems like the STAR 3 Model teach conflict resolution and communication through trust, respect, and shared goals.

- **Collaborative problem-solving strengthens culture**

  - Schools that address challenges with empathy and shared responsibility see improvements in morale and engagement.

  - Case studies from schools like the International School of Beijing and Cimarron Public School highlight how focusing on empathy, emotional support, and proactive problem-solving can drive meaningful change.

Transform Negativity

Personal Reflection

How could the new knowledge, skills, and strategies from this section impact your campus and your role?

The Energy Bus for Schools Field Guide

Refuel, Reenergize, Refocus with Purpose

When negativity is replaced with optimism, staff members experience a powerful sense of renewal. With fresh hope for the future and a renewed perspective, purpose becomes the guiding light that fuels perseverance through challenges and deepens appreciation for the journey. We don't burn out because of what we do; we burn out when we forget why we do it.

Purpose is the heart of human motivation. It gives meaning to our efforts and inspires us to rise above obstacles. When we reconnect with our purpose, we tap into an unshakable source of energy and fulfillment. That's why it's essential to rediscover it, strengthen it, and let it guide every action we take. Purpose isn't just something we have, it's something we live.

You may be in your current role in education because of a great teacher, administrator, or staff member who inspired you in the past. In Chapter 7 of *The Energy Bus for Schools* book, we highlight this in the "Gifts from the Past" section. Just as someone once lit the way for you, you now carry the torch for the next generation of educators. Purpose in teaching isn't always something people discover on their own; sometimes they need to be inspired into it. When you remember, reinforce, and root yourself in your purpose each day, you radiate that energy to others, influencing both your colleagues and students. You might even spark a desire in students to become educators themselves.

Every time I lead an Energy Bus for Schools workshop, I ask the audience how many are in education today because a teacher or staff member inspired them. Nearly 60–70% of the hands in the room go up. This shows the profound ripple effect of teaching with purpose. When you live your mission authentically and passionately, you create a legacy that inspires others to pursue their dreams and make a lasting difference.

Reflect

Think back to a time when you felt energized and motivated in your role. What specific factors fueled that sense of purpose?

____

____

____

____

____

Reflect on a challenging period in your career. How did reconnecting with your purpose, or losing sight of it, affect your ability to navigate that time?

____

____

____

____

____

Who has played a significant role in inspiring you professionally, and how did their sense of purpose shape or influence the direction of your own career?

____

____

____

____

____

What was the point you realized you were supposed to be in education? What was the light-bulb moment?

____

____

____

____

How does living with purpose impact school culture and student success?

____

____

____

____

Apply

What specific strategies can you implement to refuel your passion and stay connected to your purpose throughout the school year?

____

____

____

____

Identify one purposeful action you can take this week to inspire colleagues or students. How will this action align with the Energy Bus principles?

____

____

____

____

____

Team-Building Activities

1. Energy Bus Recharge and Refocus Stations

This activity is meant for elementary students. In order to promote team collaboration, positive mindset development, and personal reflection, students will engage in five interactive stations inspired by the principles from the book *The Energy Bus for Kids*. Each station encourages hands-on learning, group discussions, and shared experiences that reinforce core values such as positivity, teamwork, and goal-setting. This activity helps reduce stress while strengthening team dynamics through creative and meaningful tasks.

Participants will rotate through the following stations:

1. **Vision Buses:** Decorate symbolic buses with personal goals, reflecting the principle Create a Positive Vision.

2. **No Stress:** Release written worries in water to practice No Bullying Allowed.

3. **Leaping Toward Positivity:** Students use plastic leaping frogs (which can be purchased on Amazon) to leap toward a positive quote or saying. As an added element, students can measure the distance of leap to coordinate with a math lesson. This coincides with Fueling Your Ride with Positivity.

4. **Build Bridges:** Students use clean, discarded materials like old newspapers, magazines, and paper towel rolls to construct a small bridge. The bridge should be no longer than two feet and have a span high enough for a standard water

bottle to fit underneath. It must also be sturdy enough to support the weight of a full water bottle. This coincides with Love Your Passengers.

5. Group Discussion: Teams share insights from all stations, fostering a deeper understanding of Enjoy the Ride.

Each station involves practical, fun tasks designed to inspire thoughtful reflection and connection. This table shows how these activities and the Energy Bus principles come together. Note that group discussion is always the last activity for all groups to complete together.

Station Name	Activity	Energy Bus Principle
Leaping toward Positivity	Use plastic frogs to leap toward positive affirmations and discuss how they apply to life	Fuel your ride with positivity
Build Bridges	Teams collaborate to create supportive structures symbolizing how they can uplift one another	Love your passengers
Vision Buses	Participants decorate symbolic buses with personal goals	Create a positive vision
No Stress	Participants release stress by dissolving written worries in water using candies or dissolvable items	No bullying allowed
Group Discussion	Put participants in groups to discuss what they learned from each station	Enjoy the ride

2. SWAG Selection for Purpose

To foster school pride and reinforce shared purpose, small groups of four to six people will collaborate in a creative SWAG selection activity. This is an opportunity for a school to reexamine their appearance to the community. Each small group will brainstorm and design SWAG items that reflect the school's mission, vision, or key Energy Bus messages, such as "Fuel Your Ride with Positive Energy" or "Driven by Purpose."

Many schools combined key Energy Bus principles with their school's name. Teams will create short presentations explaining how their selected items promote school spirit and support staff motivation.

After all groups present, the entire staff will vote on the most impactful designs. The winning SWAG items may be ordered and distributed at a future school event. This fun, collaborative activity not only sparks creativity but also deepens staff investment in the school's culture, reminding everyone of their collective "why" while strengthening team bonds.

3. Three R's of Purpose: Remember, Reinforce, Root

In groups of two to four, educators should follow the instructions under each of the following words.

Remember

Educators should write a one- to two-sentence purpose statement here for their role and why they feel called into it.

____

____

____

____

____

Reinforce

Brainstorm one strategy to help reinforce your purpose statement on a daily basis.

____

____

____

____

____

Root

Brainstorm one strategy to stay rooted in purpose and help others to do the same.

____

____

____

____

____

4. Personal Action Plan

Create a personal action plan for reenergizing when you feel burned out. What daily or weekly practices will help you stay focused on your mission?

First, create a list of triggers that can make you feel burned out at school. Next, brainstorm daily practices you can do to help counter the feelings of burnout. In a third column, simplify your daily practice into one word to help you remember it. Use this table to help:

Triggers	Daily Practice	Daily Practice One Word
1. __________________	__________________	
__________________	__________________	
__________________	__________________	__________________
__________________	__________________	
__________________	__________________	
2. __________________	__________________	
__________________	__________________	
__________________	__________________	__________________
__________________	__________________	
__________________	__________________	

Refuel, Reenergize, Refocus with Purpose

Triggers	Daily Practice	Daily Practice One Word
3. ___________	___________	
___________	___________	
___________	___________	___________
___________	___________	
___________	___________	
4. ___________	___________	
___________	___________	
___________	___________	___________
___________	___________	
___________	___________	
5. ___________	___________	
___________	___________	
___________	___________	___________
___________	___________	
___________	___________	

5. Get in Touch

Think back to someone who inspired you, whether from your past, another school, or your current workplace. This person made a meaningful impact on your life, perhaps even influencing your decision to pursue a career in education or supporting you during your journey. Take a moment to reflect on who this person is and how they helped shape your path.

Now, brainstorm a thoughtful letter or email expressing your gratitude. Share specific ways they inspired or supported you and explain the lasting impact they've had on your life. If possible, be bold and reach out to this person directly. Letting them know how much they mattered can be a powerful and meaningful gesture, for both you and them. If they are not around anymore or you cannot get a hold of them, simply share their story or impact with others.

Case Study: Purpose-Driven Leadership in Schools

Our Certified Energy Bus Schools consistently share success stories, and one common theme behind their thriving positive cultures is the presence of purpose-driven leaders who lead with vision, intention, and energy. School leaders are the energy creators of their organizations, setting the tone and influencing the culture through their actions, attitudes, and decisions. In the face of challenges, resilient leaders support their teams by promoting emotional well-being, encouraging mental focus, and fostering inner strength. This capacity to uplift staff in difficult times stems from a shared sense of purpose, a collective belief that their work has meaning beyond day-to-day tasks. By emphasizing strengths, reinforcing trust, and encouraging collaboration, leaders cultivate a culture of optimism and empowerment, ensuring their teams rise even in adversity.

Purpose-driven leaders have energy that is contagious, igniting excitement and commitment throughout the organization.

Leaders in schools thrive not as authoritative bosses but as facilitators of growth and developers of purpose (Conley, *Roadmap to Restructuring: Policies, Practices, and the Emerging Visions of Schooling*, ERIC Clearinghouse on Educational Management, 1993). They model the behaviors they wish to see, align decisions with the school's mission, and create systems that empower staff and students alike. When leaders consistently act with integrity and purpose, they build trust and inspire loyalty. Their intentional, purpose-driven leadership transforms not only the school's culture but also its ability to adapt, excel, and sustain success over time.

Refuel, Reenergize, Refocus with Purpose

 **Best Practices and Main Takeaways**

- **Reconnect with your "why" to avoid burnout**

  - Burnout doesn't stem from the work itself but from losing sight of purpose.

  - Purpose serves as a guiding light that sustains resilience and perseverance through challenges.

  - Regular reflection on personal motivations helps maintain energy and drive.

- **Purpose is a ripple effect**

  - Living with purpose extends beyond the individual, inspiring colleagues, students, and even future educators.

  - Authentic purpose-driven actions contribute to a culture of shared vision, empowerment, and long-lasting positive impact.

- **Reflect, understand, and apply purpose daily**

  - Purpose must be remembered, reinforced, and rooted in daily actions.

  - Practices like purpose statements, reflective discussions, and action plans integrate purpose into daily school culture.

  - Purpose-driven actions influence every interaction and decision.

- **Collaborative purpose-building strengthens school culture**

  - Purpose-driven activities like team-building exercises and collaborative discussions foster unity.

  - Shared projects aligned with school values strengthen bonds within the school community.

  - Collaborative purpose-building reinforces a collective sense of mission and belonging.

The Energy Bus for Schools Field Guide

- **Leadership is by purpose-driven example**
  - School leaders are energy creators whose attitudes and actions shape the school's culture.
  - By modeling purpose-driven behavior, they promote trust, enable collaboration, and empower staff.
  - Purposeful leadership inspires teams to surpass expectations, ensuring long-term success and sustainability.

Personal Reflection

How could the new knowledge, skills, and strategies from this section impact your campus and your role?

____

Refuel, Reenergize, Refocus with Purpose

Create a Fleet of Bus Drivers to Enjoy the Ride

This guide has created meaningful opportunities for discussion, activities, and sharing about how to create a positive school culture. A positive school culture significantly influences both student achievement and staff morale. Research indicates that schools fostering shared values, high expectations, and supportive relationships create environments where students are more engaged and perform better academically. For instance, a study published in the *Shanlax International Journal of Education* found that a strong, positive school culture enhances students' academic success by promoting a sense of belonging and motivation.

Unfortunately, many schools are not positive places to work. A 2024 survey by EdChoice found that only 19% of teachers believed K–12 education was heading in the right direction nationally, marking a significant drop from previous years. Moreover, just 15% of teachers would recommend the profession to others, indicating a deepening morale crisis among educators.

While culture, fun, energy, positivity, and unity are not the sole answers to counter these trends, they are a step in the right direction. It is time to bring fun, excitement, and engagement back into schools. After I completed a professional development workshop in Oklahoma recently, the principal told me, "We have not had this much fun in a long time." School years can drag on and routines can become monotonous. That's why a big part of The Energy Bus for Schools book and this guide is to help you enjoy the ride.

Bringing fun, energy, and excitement back into Caldwell County Middle School was a top priority for their leadership. As a Certified Energy Bus School, they hosted exciting assemblies to bring everyone together. To cap off one assembly, grade levels competed for the coveted Spirit Stick, proudly displayed in the winning grade's hallway. The seventh-grade students earned the top spot, celebrating with a well-deserved dance party. This event was a perfect example of Enjoying the Ride, where fun, recognition, and positive energy came together to inspire the entire school community.

In Ohio, a small group of dedicated high school students has taken the lead in driving the Energy Bus initiative at their school, fully embracing the concept of Enjoying the Ride. Their enthusiasm shines through in creative projects that spread positivity and reinforce Energy Bus principles across campus. They've launched a TikTok page featuring weekly videos explaining Energy Bus activities, created a special section in the school newspaper for motivational quotes, and designed posters and signs during advisory class to inspire their peers.

One of their most impactful efforts has been the "Positive Post-it Challenge," where they posted encouraging notes throughout the school, inviting students to take or leave a message for someone in need of a kind word. By working closely with advisory teachers and the counseling office, this student-led team continuously finds new ways to keep Energy Bus activities fresh, fun, and meaningful while turning everyday moments into opportunities to fuel positive energy and Enjoy the Ride.

Connection Building

Reflect

After completing this field guide, what does school culture mean to you now?

____

____

____

____

____

What are the biggest challenges standing in the way of this school becoming a destination location with a positive and energized culture?

____

____

____

____

Understand

How does fostering a positive school culture impact both student success and staff morale, based on what you've learned from this field guide?

____

____

____

____

Why is it important for schools to intentionally create fun, engaging, and energizing experiences like assemblies or student-led initiatives? How can these activities influence the overall school environment?

____

____

____

____

____

Create a Fleet of Bus Drivers to Enjoy the Ride

Apply

Use the table below to reflect on your journey through this field guide. What does this work mean to you and what are your biggest takeaways from each section? Refer to this table throughout the school year.

Energy Bus Principle	What has this principle meant to you personally?	What is your biggest takeaway?
Create a Positive Vision		
Build a Positive Culture		
Fuel Your Ride with Positive Energy		

Energy Bus Principle	What has this principle meant to you personally?	What is your biggest takeaway?
Love Your Passengers		
Transform Negativity		
Refuel, Reenergize, Refocus with Purpose		
Enjoy the Ride		

Create a Fleet of Bus Drivers to Enjoy the Ride

Team-Building Activities

1. Fun Squad

In the "Build a Positive Culture" section of this field guide, we referred to the Positive School Culture Teams in schools across the country. In small groups of four to six people, brainstorm ideas for how the staff can boost comradery and fellowship to lead to an increase in belonging. This may involve after-school activities, field trips, dinners, or other fun initiatives. If you have a Positive School Culture Team on campus, make sure they have these ideas for planning and execution. It's time to bring fun, friendship, and togetherness back into our schools.

____

____

____

____

2. Celebrate Campus Wins

Take a moment to reflect on and list all the great things happening on campus. Independently, everyone should create their own list, then collaborate in small groups of 4–6 people, to compile a shared list. Finally, the entire group will come together to create a master list on flipchart paper displayed at the front of the room. This exercise is a chance to slow down, appreciate both the big and small successes happening on campus, and recognize the positive momentum already in place. Conclude by brainstorming ways to share these accomplishments with the broader school community. Be sure to read about a related activity called the "Good News Jar" in the Additional Case Study and Resources section toward the end of this book.

____

____

____

____

3. *Positivity Notebook*

This idea gained momentum when Hephzibah High School in Georgia, a Certified Energy Bus School, implemented it a few years ago to boost staff morale. They purchased a simple spiral notebook and labeled it the Positivity Notebook. If the notebook appeared in your staff mailbox, it meant someone had written you a note of encouragement or positivity. The recipient's task was then to pay it forward by writing a positive note to another staff member and placing the notebook in their mailbox. The impact was so profound that the notebook made its way to the district office, inspiring multiple "Positivity Notebooks" to spring up across the district, spreading encouragement far beyond the school's walls.

To bring this tradition to your school, start the Positivity Notebook and let it circulate across campus. Encourage staff to keep the chain of positivity going throughout the school year, creating a lasting culture of encouragement, support, and gratitude. Let the power of paying it forward inspire and uplift your entire school community.

____

____

____

4. *Create a Plan for Fun Student Assemblies*

Assemblies can be a fun and exciting experience for students. Central Boulevard Elementary in New York, another Certified Energy Bus School, has created impactful experiences for their students through assemblies. They typically hold assemblies for each Energy Bus for Schools principle and use music, games, interaction, dancing, speeches, and more. Begin the process for drafting what different assemblies can look like on campus. These assemblies can be based on the principles from *The Energy Bus for Kids* book, which are applicable to all school levels.

Review of the principles from *The Energy Bus for Kids*:

1. Create a Positive Vision

2. Fuel Your Ride with Positive Energy

Create a Fleet of Bus Drivers to Enjoy the Ride

3. No Bullying Allowed

4. Love Your Passengers

5. Enjoy the Ride

In small groups of four to six people, assign each group one of *The Energy Bus for Kids* principles. If there are more than five groups, continue assigning principles to multiple groups as needed. Each group should brainstorm and design an assembly tailored to the ages at your school, incorporating elements like music, activities, lessons to share, awards, and ways to encourage staff and student interaction.

After generating their ideas, reconvene as a full staff to share and discuss each group's concepts. Together, create a master plan for assemblies based on all five principles, or establish an assembly committee to refine the ideas and develop a cohesive plan.

We have seen schools post about engaging assemblies by having a staff karaoke or lip-sync battle featuring upbeat songs related to Enjoy the Ride themes. These schools have encouraged participation by creating teams or performing as grade-level groups. They have made it even more fun by incorporating costumes or props. It's all about creating memories and energy as the school year goes on.

____

____

____

____

____

5. Positivity Relay Challenge

This activity is designed to promote team spirit and spread positivity through fun, active participation. First, divide staff into teams of four to six people and set up relay-style challenges. Each station features a task inspired by an Energy Bus principle, such as writing an encouraging note to a colleague or sharing a positive classroom moment. After completing all tasks, teams reflect on how these small acts can fuel positivity on campus.

1. **Create a Positive Vision (Goal Post-it Wall)**

   - *Task:* Each participant writes one goal or positive vision for the school on a sticky note and places it on a "Vision Wall." Teams cheer when a new Post-it is added.

   - *Example:* "Our school will be a place where every student feels supported and valued."

2. **Fuel Your Ride with Positive Energy (Encouragement Notes)**

   - *Task:* Write a quick encouraging note or positive affirmation to a colleague or student. Place it in a designated "Fuel Box" or deliver it later.

   - *Example:* "You're making a huge difference every day. Keep up the amazing work!"

3. **No Bullying Allowed (Positive Pep Talk)**

   - *Task:* Role-play a quick, supportive "pep talk" with a partner. One person pretends to be having a tough day, and the other delivers an uplifting message to lift their spirits. Switch roles and repeat.

   - *Example:* "I know today has been challenging, but you've got this! You're stronger than any obstacle you face."

4. **Love Your Passengers (Acts of Kindness Challenge)**

   - *Task:* Teams brainstorm five simple acts of kindness they can complete that week. Share one idea aloud with a facilitator before moving on.

   - *Example:* "Compliment three people today" or "Leave a positive note on a colleague's desk."

5. **Enjoy the Ride (Gratitude Chain)**

   - *Task:* Each person writes something they're grateful for about the school or a colleague on a paper strip. Connect these strips to make links, turning them into a "Gratitude Chain" that grows throughout the activity.

   - *Example:* "I'm thankful for our supportive admin team and collaborative teachers."

Create a Fleet of Bus Drivers to Enjoy the Ride

Case Study: Break the Walls Down at Bellflower Elementary

Bellflower Elementary, in Ohio, has embraced a "no walls" learning environment since the 1970s, creating a truly unique school culture. During a recent staff development workshop, I was struck by the school's open design. Each grade level occupies its own cluster, with low bookshelves serving as the only dividers between classrooms. Teacher desks are arranged in clusters to encourage communication and collaboration. This setup fosters a culture where teachers team-teach, align schedules, and coordinate lessons, making learning both dynamic and interconnected.

The positive energy on campus is palpable. Staff members are welcoming, supportive, and committed to their shared mission. Their principal, a strong advocate for the Energy Bus approach, integrates its principles into staff collaboration and schoolwide initiatives. A standout example is their "Energy Bus Ticket" program, where students earn tickets for positive behavior. These tickets are posted onto a large, decorated paper bus on display, symbolizing the collective effort toward creating a positive school culture. In one school year, the school surpassed 2,800 tickets, a record they're determined to beat again. The open-concept environment drives communication, builds strong relationships, and reinforces a sense of shared purpose, helping staff and students truly Enjoy the Ride.

At Merritt High School, a Certified Energy Bus School, creating a culture where both students and staff *Enjoy the Ride* has been the driving force behind a vibrant and energized campus. This year, a variety of activities were launched to maintain high energy levels and foster positive connections. One initiative, the "Positive Mailbox," allows students and staff to submit uplifting messages that are shared during weekly intercom announcements. Music now fills the commons area, where students gather each morning and during lunch, setting a welcoming and upbeat tone for the day. Another creative touch is the "High School Fridge," where

(continued)

Create a Fleet of Bus Drivers to Enjoy the Ride

exceptional responses and standout classroom work from the weekly Energy Bus for Schools program activities are proudly displayed, reinforcing positive achievements in a fun and visible way.

Engagement extends to exciting campus-wide events like the "Snowball Fight," where students write down negative thoughts, wad them into "snowballs," and symbolically toss them away in a fun, interactive hallway activity. This hands-on event encourages students to release negative emotions and start the new year with a fresh mindset. Staff also experience this culture of positivity through the school's Energy Bus staff committee. Open to anyone interested in contributing ideas, the committee has grown significantly, requiring extra seating at meetings, a testament to the staff's commitment to the program. Additionally, monthly surveys help keep a pulse on staff well-being, ensuring concerns are addressed promptly and individually.

The school's focus on recognizing and celebrating positive contributions further drives its mission. Each month, staff members vote for an "Energy Bus Driver of the Month," honoring peers who embody Energy Bus principles. Winners receive a thoughtful gift, a special announcement, and recognition on the school's social media platforms. By combining intentional, inclusive activities with meaningful recognition, Merritt High School has created a thriving community where everyone feels connected, valued, and motivated to *Enjoy the Ride* together.

The Energy Bus for Schools Field Guide

 **Best Practices and Main Takeaways**

- **Foster a positive school culture**

  - A positive school culture boosts student engagement, staff morale, and academic success.

  - Schools must focus on shared values, high expectations, and supportive relationships to build lasting success.

- **Lead with fun, energy, and engagement**

  - Infusing fun into school activities creates an environment where students and staff stay motivated.

  - Hosting events like spirit assemblies, fun competitions, and interactive student-led projects drives engagement and positive energy.

- **Empower student and staff leadership**

  - Schools thrive when students and staff take ownership of schoolwide initiatives.

  - Leadership teams can organize projects like "Positive Post-it Challenges" and energy-filled assemblies to promote a culture of responsibility and positivity.

- **Recognize and celebrate success**

  - Recognizing students and staff through awards like "Energy Bus Driver of the Month" or showcasing achievements on social media boosts morale.

  - Public celebrations of success reinforce positive behavior and create a strong, united school community.

- **Commit to continuous culture-building**

  - Creating a culture of positivity requires ongoing efforts through professional development, fun squads, and reflective practices.

  - Schools can strengthen community bonds through team-building activities, such as staff karaoke battles or collaborative school projects, ensuring long-term cultural success.

Create a Fleet of Bus Drivers to Enjoy the Ride

Personal Reflection

How could the new knowledge, skills, and strategies from this section impact your campus and your role?

____

____

____

____

____

Additional Case Studies

Case Study: Rebuilding Through Positivity: A School's Journey on the Energy Bus

A school I recently worked with, after experiencing the unimaginable loss of a student, recognized the urgent need to unite its community. They sought a shared purpose that would connect students, faculty, parents, and community members to the school's mission while fostering healing. Believing that positivity could be the driving force for change, the school became a Certified Energy Bus School, committing to strengthening relationships and building a supportive culture. Through access to weekly Energy Bus activities, they aimed to infuse life, meaningful conversations, and renewed energy into their campus.

While no program can erase the pain of losing a student, the school chose to move forward with hope, honoring the student's legacy by focusing on positive mental health and community support. They provided students with activities designed to encourage self-reflection and meaningful interactions. Following impactful student assemblies, featured in the "Transforming Negativity" section, the school began to rise with renewed strength and purpose. Their mission now centers on cultivating positivity, inclusivity, and growth to produce lasting, positive outcomes. Today, they are fully on the Energy Bus, driven by purpose and fueled by hope.

Case Study: Fueling Positivity: Simple Strategies That Transform School Culture

At Dixon High School, one of the first Certified Energy Bus High Schools, they launched an initiative called "Fuel Your Ride" Notes as part of their efforts to create a positive and connected school culture. They designated a central location where students could pick up these notes, write messages of encouragement, and place them in a symbolic school bus. At random times, the principal would pull notes from the bus and personally deliver them to the recipients. This became one of the principal's favorite responsibilities. Whether presenting these notes to staff or students in their classrooms, the heartfelt recognition often led to applause and celebration, fostering a truly uplifting atmosphere.

In addition to the "Fuel Your Ride" Notes, they introduced "Positivity Tickets" to celebrate student achievements. Staff members would fill out Energy Bus slips for positive office referrals, which administrators used to recognize students by presenting certificates, making positive phone calls home, and highlighting their accomplishments on social media platforms. These small yet meaningful acts of recognition helped build a culture of appreciation and reinforced positive behavior across the school.

(continued)

Additional Case Studies

These strategies have been so impactful that the principal, Steve Clarke, continued using them at other schools, including in his current role as principal at Richlands High School in North Carolina. The Positivity Tickets remain a cornerstone of their efforts to create an encouraging environment where students and staff alike feel seen, supported, and celebrated.

Case Study: A Legacy of Love and Leadership

At the Gertrude Walden Day Care Center in Stuart, Florida, Thelma Washington has been transforming the lives of students and staff for decades. Despite being in an underserved community, the center has become a beacon of hope and positivity for local families.

Each Thanksgiving, the center raises funds, recruits volunteers, and prepares hundreds of Thanksgiving meals for the community. Residents can simply drive by and receive a delicious meal at no cost. Thelma not only leads these efforts but also inspires her staff and volunteers to serve with open hearts and joyful spirits, teaching valuable cooking skills along the way. This beautiful tradition has become something the entire community eagerly anticipates each year.

As the executive director, Thelma oversees a bustling school that serves toddlers through VPK (Voluntary Prekindergarten) students. Her responsibilities are significant, overseeing multiple classrooms and supporting a high-needs student body. Yet she cultivates a team of dedicated staff members, many of whom have stayed for over 20 years, an impressive feat in early childhood education. When asked how she's achieved this, Thelma was clear: She prioritizes loving and appreciating her staff. She goes out of her way to show gratitude through small yet meaningful gestures, such as covering a classroom to give someone an extended lunch break, giving gift cards or flowers, and spending quality time with each team member to ensure they feel truly valued. However, she balances this care with high expectations, holding her staff accountable to bring their best and most positive selves to work each day.

Thelma's impact extends far beyond her staff. Former students often return to volunteer or donate to the center, grateful for the foundation it gave them. One notable former student even went on to attend Harvard University and remains in touch with her to this day. Thelma's leadership is a reminder that small, intentional acts of kindness, when paired with a heart dedicated to service, can transform not only a school but an entire community.

Powering Up: Connecting Your School to The Energy Bus

This section includes additional activities and resources for you to use to introduce and reinforce ideas from *The Energy Bus for Schools* into your institution.

Aligning Current School Practices with *The Energy Bus for Schools*

In this activity, you will explore how your current school systems, practices, and initiatives align with *The Energy Bus for Schools* principles. Begin by reviewing the main principles and reflecting on how they connect to your daily work. In small groups, you'll be assigned two or three principles and brainstorm examples of existing school routines, programs, or strategies that reflect these principles. Write each example on a sticky note. Consider how your teaching methods, classroom management strategies, or schoolwide initiatives already support positive culture and success.

Next, gather as a team to create a visual display of *The Energy Bus for Schools* principles. Present your sticky notes and place them in the corresponding sections of the display. If some examples overlap multiple principles, place multiple sticky notes on the display. Afterward, discuss common themes, strengths, and areas where intentional improvement could enhance alignment. To close the activity, choose one action you will continue or strengthen in your role, write it on a "bus ticket," and sign it as a commitment to driving positive change in the school community.

Here is a reminder of The Energy Bus for Schools principles:

- Invite Others on the Bus

- Build a Positive Culture

- Fuel Your Ride with Positive Energy

- Love Your Passengers

- Transform Negativity

- Refuel, Reenergize, and Refocus with Purpose

- Create a Fleet of Bus Drivers

The Good News Jar

One family we know uses a creative and uplifting approach to document the positive events that happen throughout the year. As good things occur, whether small wins, memorable moments, or major accomplishments, family members write them down on slips of paper and place them in a large jar kept in a central spot for all to see. On New Year's Eve, the family gathers to read through the notes, reflecting on the positive experiences and memories that shaped their year. This tradition not only celebrates success but also encourages meaningful conversations about growth and aspirations for the coming year.

Unlike the common approach of focusing solely on past shortcomings and resolutions to "fix" them, this practice prioritizes positivity while still acknowledging areas for improvement. It serves as a refreshing reminder that growth begins with gratitude and recognition of achievements, big or small.

As a school, you can adopt this idea to foster a positive culture among staff and students. Place a "Good News Jar" in visible areas, such as the front office, staff lounge, or individual classrooms, and encourage everyone to contribute notes highlighting their positive experiences throughout the year.

By making positivity a shared focus, this activity can inspire reflection, celebrate progress, and strengthen your school community's collective mindset, one good news story at a time.

Staff Engagement Survey Results

These survey results from our Certified Energy Bus Schools on how to engage with staff members feature diverse ideas on how to foster staff connections and improve morale. Responses range from providing unstructured time and food for organic interactions to hosting structured activities that encourage team-building.

- **Organic Connection and Personal Time:** Many suggest avoiding forced activities and instead providing time for teachers to work in their rooms, extended lunch breaks, or casual gatherings with food.

- **Simple Appreciation Activities:** Ideas include writing notes of appreciation, "connection cards" with conversation prompts, or personal notes from leaders.

- **Interactive Team-Building:** Recommendations include friendly competitions like *Shark Tank*-type presentations, scavenger hunts, and vision boards.

- **Mindfulness and Reflection:** Activities such as "choose a word for the new year" bracelets and peace circles were highlighted for promoting mindfulness and intention-setting.

- **Food and Treats:** Providing snacks, breakfast, or a snack bar was frequently mentioned as a way to foster informal conversations.

- **Creative Icebreakers:** Ideas like trivia or *The Amazing Race* were noted for sparking fun interactions.

- **Room for Reflection:** Some respondents emphasized skipping games and providing teachers with more time and autonomy.

The key is to understand your staff best and what they need at key moments. There may be times when autonomy and simple catch-up time in the classroom is needed. However, there may also be a time when the staff needs to come together, have fun, collaborate, and separate from school-related work and discussions. Don't be afraid to bring fun into your campus.

Fueling Relationships: The Power of Listening and Expression Awareness

Strong communication skills are the foundation of every successful relationship, and a crucial part of being a great communicator is mastering the art of listening. In today's fast-paced and distracted world, honing our listening abilities is more important than ever. Remember, listening is a mental and intentional process, while hearing is a physical one.

To reinforce effective listening behaviors, introduce your staff or team to the acronym SOLER, which serves as a guide for how we should position ourselves when listening to someone:

S—Seated: Sit in a stable, attentive position.

O—Open: Maintain open, non-defensive body language, facing the speaker.

L—Lean: Lean slightly forward to show interest.

E—Eyes: Maintain appropriate eye contact to stay engaged.

R—Relax: Stay calm and focused, showing that you are mentally present.

Listening versus Hearing: A Communication Skills Activity

Activity Instructions:

1. **Pair or Group Formation:** Divide participants into pairs or groups of three. In a trio, assign two as "listeners" and one as the "speaker." In a pair, one person will be the speaker and the other will be the listener.

2. **Storytelling:** The speaker shares a personal, emotional story or meaningful experience.

3. **Active Disruption:** As the speaker tells their story, the listener(s) will intentionally break the SOLER guidelines one at a time (e.g., shifting body language, avoiding eye contact). This disruption will likely challenge the speaker's focus and flow.

4. **Debrief:** After one minute, pause the exercise and discuss the experience. Ask the speaker how they felt and the listeners how they perceived their role.

5. **Redo with Intention:** Reassign roles if desired and repeat the exercise, this time encouraging all participants to follow all SOLER behaviors.

6. **Final Reflection:** Debrief again to discuss how effective listening impacts communication and emotional connection.

By practicing and reflecting on these listening skills, participants will gain a deeper appreciation for the role of active listening in fostering connection and understanding.

Recognizing Universal Facial Expressions

Dr. Paul Ekman's research into facial expressions and body language identified seven universal emotions expressed through distinct facial cues:

1. **Happiness:** Raised cheeks, crow's feet around the eyes, and a smile
2. **Sadness:** Drooping eyelids, downturned mouth corners, and raised inner eyebrows
3. **Fear:** Raised eyebrows, widened eyes, and slightly open mouth
4. **Anger:** Furrowed brows, narrowed eyes, and a tight, pressed mouth
5. **Surprise:** Raised eyebrows, wide-open eyes, and an open mouth
6. **Disgust:** Wrinkled nose, raised upper lip, and squinted eyes
7. **Contempt:** Slight smirk or asymmetrical tightening of one side of the mouth

Instructions:

1. Write each of the seven facial expressions on separate cards, fold them, and call for seven volunteers to come to the front of the room.
2. Hand each volunteer a folded card containing one facial expression.
3. Explain the task: Each volunteer will say the phrase "I need to see you in my office right away," using their assigned facial expression and body language to convey the emotion.
4. One at a time, each volunteer performs their line while the audience guesses which emotion they are portraying.

Debrief:

Discuss how subtle differences in body language and facial expressions can change the entire meaning of a message. Reflect on the importance of being mindful of nonverbal communication in everyday interactions.

This activity helps participants become more aware of nonverbal cues and the impact they have on emotional interpretation.

What's Next

🎉 You Made It! Now Let's Keep the Energy Going!

Congratulations on completing the field guide! Whether you journeyed solo or as a team, we know you're fired up and ready to create real change.

Now what?

☑ Reflect

☑ Plan

☑ Take action

Let's build something lasting and meaningful for your entire school community.

🚌 Join the Energy Bus for Schools Program

Become a Certified Energy Bus School!

Bring positivity to life with our five simple rules adapted from the book:

1. Create a Positive Vision

2. Fuel Your Ride with Positivity

3. No Bullies Allowed

4. Love Your Passengers

5. Enjoy the Ride

What's Included:

✓ Weekly grade-level activities

✓ Monthly leadership coaching

✓ Posters, printables, and fun schoolwide challenges

✓ Ongoing support from our team

✓ Parent resources to engage with The Energy Bus rules at home

🔥 Schools across the country are transforming culture with this program. **Yours can, too.**

☞ Visit EnergyBusForSchools.com or scan the QR code to learn more!

🎤 Want to Be a Certified Speaker or Trainer?

Dream of leading workshops or keynotes based on Jon Gordon's books:

☑ *The Energy Bus*
☑ *The Power of Positive Leadership*
☑ *The Power of a Positive Team*

We'll equip you with:

✓ All slide decks and materials
✓ Online resource library
✓ Coaching and support
✓ Optional *Energy Bus for Schools* add-on certification

Create Impact and Income!

☞ Visit JonGordonCertified.com or *scan the QR code to apply today!*

🎤 Have Us Speak to Your Campus or District

Looking to energize your team, strengthen school culture, and inspire lasting change? **Our Energy Bus for Schools team delivers powerful, interactive experiences** that leave a lasting impact.

We offer:
- ☑ Staff professional development (half or full day)
- ☑ District-wide keynotes and convocations
- ☑ Leadership and administrator workshops
- ☑ Student assemblies and classroom visits

With decades of combined experience, our speakers use stories, music, laughter, and proven strategies to inspire positive transformation.

Let us help you energize your entire school community.

☞ Find out how to bring this experience to your school: energybusforschools.com/contact/ or scan the QR code.

🎧 Listen to the *Energy Bus for Schools* Podcast

Get a regular dose of positivity and practical tips!

Listen to the *Energy Bus for Schools* podcast to reenergize your mindset, boost your leadership, and transform your school culture!

Each episode delivers:

☑ Real stories from educators and school leaders

☑ Strategies that are working in classrooms and campuses right now

☑ Fresh ideas for building a positive, connected, and resilient school culture

☑ Encouragement to keep you fueled and focused—especially on the tough days

Whether you're a principal, teacher, coach, or support staff, this podcast is your on-the-go professional development with heart.

🎙 *Short. Powerful. Uplifting.*

☞ *Scan the QR code or visit EnergyBusForSchools.com/podcast to start listening today!*

✉ Get the Positive Educator Newsletter

Stay connected. Stay inspired.

Our *Positive Educator* newsletter delivers encouragement, ideas, and resources straight to your inbox—designed to help you lead with purpose and positivity every single week.

What you'll get:

☑ Culture-building strategies you can use immediately

☑ Success stories from other Energy Bus Schools

☑ Exclusive tools, challenges, and downloads

☑ First access to upcoming trainings, events, and opportunities

☑ A dose of encouragement and practical wisdom to fuel your journey

Whether you're a classroom teacher, campus leader, or district decision-maker, this is your go-to source for continuous growth and inspiration.

☞ *Scan the QR code or sign up now at EnergyBusForSchools.com to stay in the loop!*

About the Authors

Jon Gordon is an 19-time bestselling author and one of the most influential and sought-after leadership experts and speakers today. He's a consultant to numerous leaders, CEOs, championship coaches and teams, and high performers. He impacts millions of people each year with his books, talks, podcasts, and messages.

His mission is to develop Positive Leaders who make a positive impact in every business, school, team, organization, and community to create a more positive world.

Dr. Jim Van Allan is the president of the Energy Bus for Schools program, which gives schools the blueprint and framework to create a positive school culture. He coaches school leaders and superintendents on mindset, teamwork, communication, and culture-building. Additionally, Jim speaks to schools and districts across the country with keynotes, trainings, workshops, and student assemblies. He is the coauthor, with Jon Gordon, of the *USA Today* bestselling book *The Energy Bus for Schools*.

Jim is also a professor of communication studies and lead speech instructor with Keiser University, which is based in Florida. He teaches public speaking, interpersonal communication, and business communication.

He runs *The Energy Bus for Schools* podcast and helps with a charity YouTube channel called the Fitness Mission. Jim lives in Palm City, Florida, with his wife and their three children, Brady, Brenden, and Brinley. You can follow him on social media: @JimVanAllan on all platforms.

Other Books by Jon Gordon

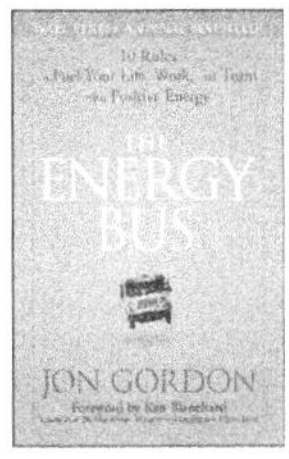

The Energy Bus

A man whose life and career are in shambles learns from a unique bus driver and set of passengers how to overcome adversity. Enjoy an enlightening ride of positive energy that is improving the way leaders lead, employees work, and teams function. **www.TheEnergyBus.com**

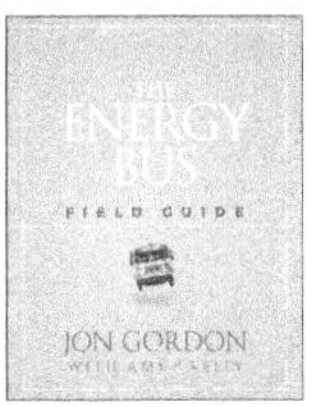

The Energy Bus Field Guide

Jon Gordon's international bestseller, *The Energy Bus,* has inspired thousands of businesses, organizations, sport teams, schools, and families alike, helping them cultivate positive energy, overcome adversity, and bring out the best in themselves and those around them. *The Energy Bus Field Guide* is a simple and powerful guide for putting *The Energy Bus* lessons to work. Using the 10 principles, you'll discover how to navigate the twists and turns that often sabotage individual and team success, and how to move in the right direction with vision, focus, purpose, and positive energy.

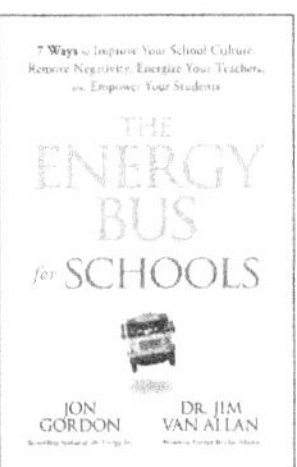

The Energy Bus for Schools

Based on *The Energy Bus,* the *Wall Street Journal* bestseller by lead author Jon Gordon, *The Energy Bus for Schools* teaches educators how to fuel their schools, themselves, and their students with positive energy. Research shows that culture and leadership greatly influence a school's learning environment and students' academic success. This book will help teachers work together to create a school culture where school leaders and students can grow into positive leaders, energizing their school culture as a united front.

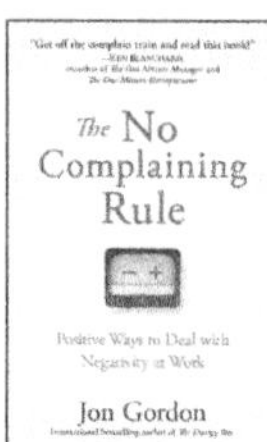

The No Complaining Rule

Follow a vice president of human resources who must save herself and her company from ruin and discover proven principles and an actionable plan to win the battle against individual and organizational negativity.
www.NoComplainingRule.com

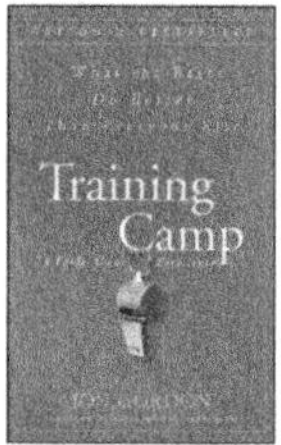

Training Camp

This inspirational story about a small guy with a big heart, and a special coach who guides him on a quest for excellence, reveals the 11 winning habits that separate the best individuals and teams from the rest.
www.TrainingCamp11.com

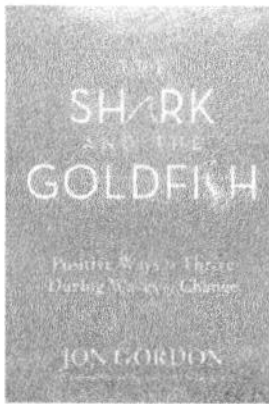

The Shark and the Goldfish

Delightfully illustrated, this quick read is packed with tips and strategies on how to respond to challenges beyond your control in order to thrive during waves of change.
www.SharkandGoldfish.com

Soup

The newly appointed CEO of a popular soup company is brought in to reinvigorate the brand and bring success back to a company that has fallen on hard times. Through her journey, discover the key ingredients to unite, engage, and inspire teams to create a culture of greatness.
www.Soup11.com

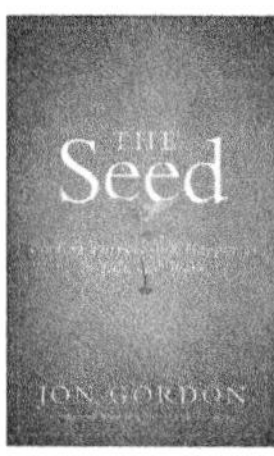

The Seed

Go on a quest for the meaning and passion behind work with Josh, an up-and-comer at his company who is disenchanted with his job. Through Josh's cross-country journey, you'll find surprising new sources of wisdom and inspiration in your own business and life.
www.Seed11.com

Other Books by Jon Gordon

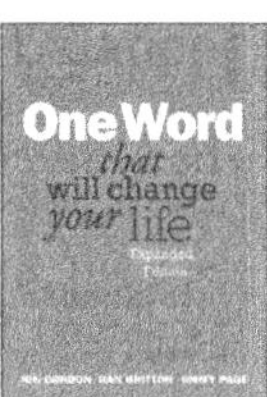

One Word

One Word is a simple concept that delivers powerful life change! This quick read will inspire you to simplify your life and work by focusing on just one word for this year. *One Word* creates clarity, power, passion, and life-change. When you find your word, live it, and share it, your life will become more rewarding and exciting than ever.
www.getoneword.com

The Positive Dog

We all have two dogs inside of us. One dog is positive, happy, optimistic, and hopeful. The other dog is negative, mad, pessimistic, and fearful. These two dogs often fight inside us, but guess who wins? The one you feed the most. *The Positive Dog* is an inspiring story that not only reveals the strategies and benefits of being positive, but also an essential truth: being positive doesn't just make you better; it makes everyone around you better.
www.feedthepositivedog.com

The Carpenter

The Carpenter is Jon Gordon's most inspiring book yet—filled with powerful lessons and success strategies. Michael wakes up in the hospital with a bandage on his head and fear in his heart after collapsing during a morning jog. When Michael finds out the man who saved his life is a carpenter, he visits him and quickly learns that he is more than just a carpenter; he is also a builder of lives, careers, people, and teams. In this journey, you will learn timeless principles to help you stand out, excel, and make an impact on people and the world.
www.carpenter11.com

The Hard Hat

A true story about Cornell lacrosse player George Boiardi, *The Hard Hat* is an unforgettable book about a selfless, loyal, joyful, hard-working, competitive, and compassionate leader and teammate, the impact he had on his team and program, and the lessons we can learn from him. This inspirational story will teach you how to build a great team and be the best teammate you can be.
www.hardhat21.com

Other Books by Jon Gordon

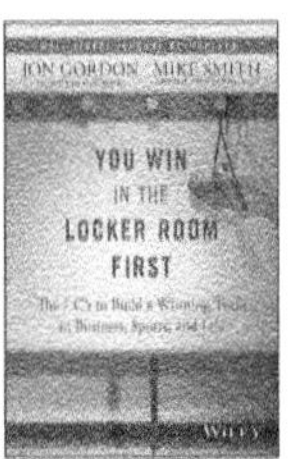

You Win in the Locker Room First

Based on the extraordinary experiences of NFL Coach Mike Smith and leadership expert Jon Gordon, *You Win in the Locker Room First* offers a rare, behind-the-scenes look at one of the most pressure-packed leadership jobs on the planet, and what leaders can learn from these experiences in order to build their own winning teams.
www.wininthelockerroom.com

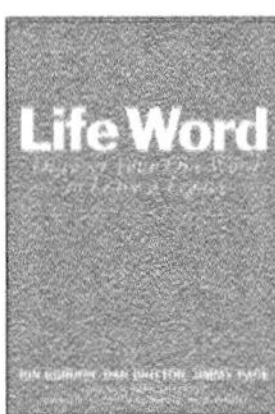

Life Word

Life Word reveals a simple, powerful tool to help you identify the word that will inspire you to live your best life while leaving your greatest legacy. In the process, you'll discover your *why*, which will help show you how to live with a renewed sense of power, purpose, and passion.
www.getoneword.com/lifeword

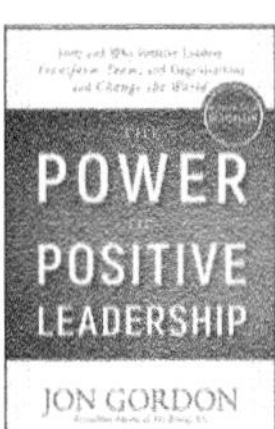

The Power of Positive Leadership

The Power of Positive Leadership is your personal coach for becoming the leader your people deserve. Jon Gordon gathers insights from his bestselling fables to bring you the definitive guide to positive leadership. Difficult times call for leaders who are up to the challenge. Results are the by-product of your culture, teamwork, vision, talent, innovation, execution, and commitment. This book shows you how to bring it all together to become a powerfully positive leader.
www.powerofpositiveleadership.com

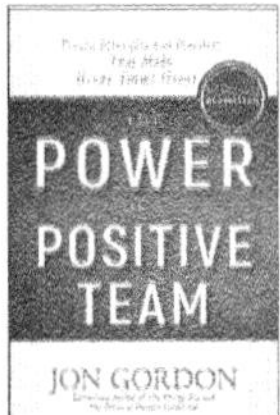

The Power of a Positive Team

In *The Power of a Positive Team*, Jon Gordon draws on his unique team-building experience, as well as conversations with some of the greatest teams in history, to provide an essential framework of proven practices to empower teams to work together more effectively and achieve superior results.
www.PowerOfAPositiveTeam.com

The Coffee Bean

From bestselling author Jon Gordon and rising star Damon West comes *The Coffee Bean*: an illustrated fable that teaches readers how to transform their environment, overcome challenges, and create positive change.
www.coffeebeanbook.com

Other Books by Jon Gordon

Stay Positive

Fuel yourself and others with positive energy—inspirational quotes and encouraging messages to live by from bestselling author Jon Gordon. Keep this little book by your side, read from it each day, and feed your mind, body, and soul with the power of positivity.
www.StayPositiveBook.com

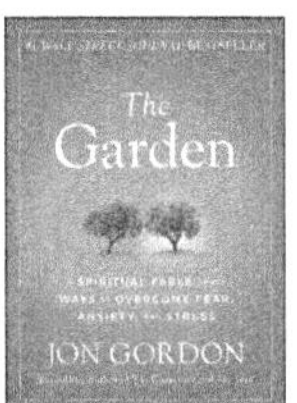

The Garden

The Garden is an enlightening and encouraging fable that helps readers overcome the 5 D's (doubt, distortion, discouragement, distractions, and division) in order to find more peace, focus, connection, and happiness. Jon tells a story of teenage twins who, through the help of a neighbor and his special garden, find ancient wisdom, life-changing lessons, and practical strategies to overcome the fear, anxiety, and stress in their lives.
www.readthegarden.com

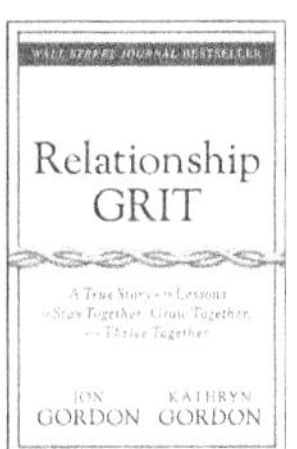

Relationship Grit

Bestselling author Jon Gordon is back with another life-affirming book. This time, he teams up with Kathryn Gordon, his wife of 23 years, for a look at what it takes to build strong relationships. In *Relationship Grit*, the Gordons reveal what brought them together, what kept them together through difficult times, and what continues to sustain their love and passion for one another to this day.
www.relationshipgritbook.com

Stick Together

From bestselling author Jon Gordon and coauthor Kate Leavell, *Stick Together* delivers a crucial message about the power of belief, ownership, connection, love, inclusion, consistency, and hope. The authors guide individuals and teams on an inspiring journey to show them how to persevere through challenges, overcome obstacles, and create success together.
www.sticktogetherbook.com

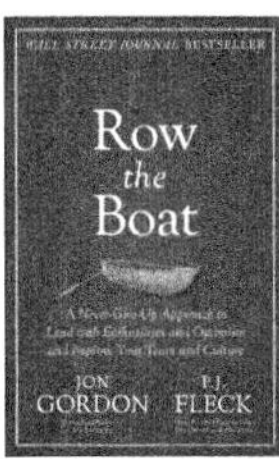

Row the Boat

In *Row the Boat*, Minnesota Golden Gophers Head Coach P.J. Fleck and bestselling author Jon Gordon deliver an inspiring message about what you can achieve when you approach life with a never-give-up philosophy. The book shows you how to choose enthusiasm and optimism as your guiding lights instead of being defined by circumstances and events outside of your control.
www.rowtheboatbook.com

Other Books by Jon Gordon

The Sale

In *The Sale*, bestselling author Jon Gordon and rising star Alex Demczak deliver an invaluable lesson about what matters most in life and work and how to achieve it. The book teaches four lessons about integrity in order to create lasting success.
www.thesalebook.com

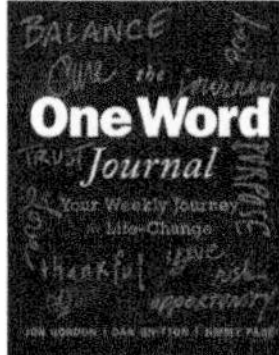

The One Word Journal

In *The One Word Journal*, bestselling authors Jon Gordon, Dan Britton, and Jimmy Page deliver a powerful new approach to simplifying and transforming your life and business. You'll learn how to access the core of your intention every week of the year as you explore 52 weekly lessons, principles, and wins that unleash the power of your One Word.

How to Be a Coffee Bean

In *How to Be a Coffee Bean*, bestselling coauthors of *The Coffee Bean*, Jon Gordon and Damon West, present 111 simple and effective strategies to help you lead a coffee bean lifestyle—one full of healthy habits, encouragement, and genuine happiness. From athletes to students and executives, countless individuals have been inspired by *The Coffee Bean* message. Now, *How to Be a Coffee Bean* teaches you how to put *The Coffee Bean* philosophy into action to help you create real and lasting change in your life.

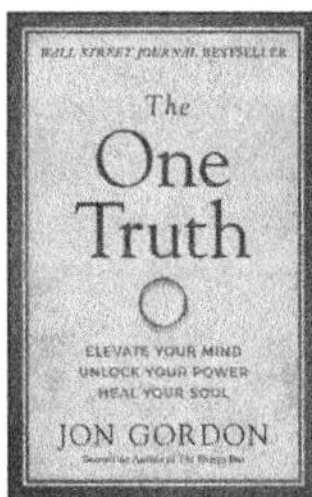

The One Truth

In *The One Truth*, bestselling author and thought leader Jon Gordon guides you on a path to discover revolutionary insights, ancient truths, and practical strategies to elevate your mind, unlock your power, and live life to the fullest. Once you know the One Truth, you'll see how it impacts leadership, teamwork, mindset, performance, relationships, addictions, social media, anxiety, mental health, healing, and ultimately determines what you create and experience.

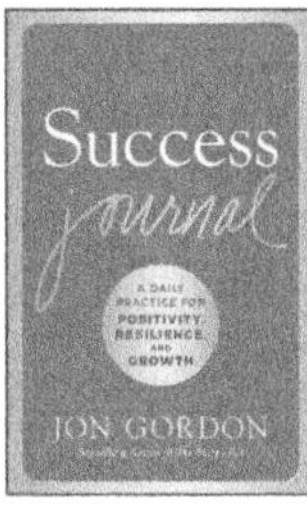

Success Journal

Success Journal: A Daily Practice for Positivity, Resilience, and Growth is a daily, lined journal where readers can write down their success of the day, shift their nighttime focus from negativity to positivity, and thereby create more success and opportunities in their lives. This resource is inspired by the legendary Bart Connor, who credited his overcoming a torn bicep muscle to win two gold medals at the 1984 Olympics to his parents asking him about his success of the day as a child.

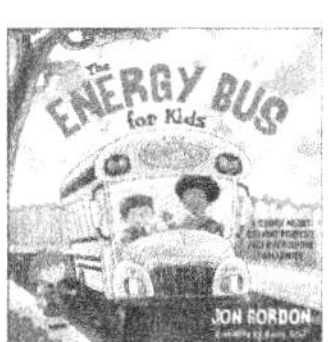

The Energy Bus for Kids

The illustrated children's adaptation of the bestselling book *The Energy Bus* tells the story of George, who, with the help of his school bus driver, Joy, learns that if he believes in himself, he'll find the strength to overcome any challenge. His journey teaches kids how to overcome negativity, bullies, and everyday challenges to be their best.
www.EnergyBusKids.com

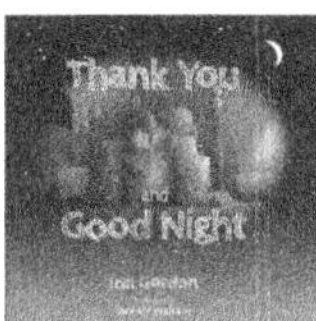

Thank You and Good Night

Thank You and Good Night is a beautifully illustrated book that shares the heart of gratitude. Jon Gordon takes a little boy and girl on a fun-filled journey from one perfect moonlit night to the next. During their adventurous days and nights, the children explore the people, places, and things they are thankful for.

The Hard Hat for Kids

The Hard Hat for Kids is an illustrated guide to teamwork. Adapted from the bestseller *The Hard Hat*, this uplifting story presents practical insights and life-changing lessons that are immediately applicable to everyday situations, giving kids—and adults—a new outlook on cooperation, friendship, and the selfless nature of true teamwork.
www.HardHatforKids.com

One Word for Kids

If you could choose only one word to help you have your best year ever, what would it be? *Love? Fun? Believe? Brave?* It's probably different for each person. How you find your word is just as important as the word itself. And once you know your word, what do you do with it? In *One Word for Kids,* bestselling author Jon Gordon—along with coauthors Dan Britton and Jimmy Page—asks these questions to children and adults of all ages, teaching an important life lesson in the process.
www.getoneword.com/kids

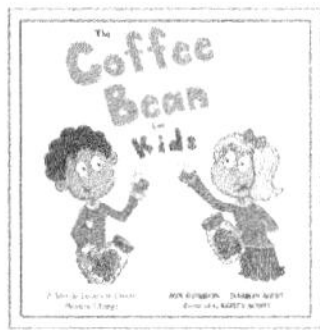

The Coffee Bean for Kids

The bestselling authors of *The Coffee Bean* inspire and encourage children with this transformative tale of personal strength. Perfect for parents, teachers, and children who wish to overcome negativity and challenging situations, *The Coffee Bean for Kids* teaches readers about the potential that each one of us has to lead, influence, and make a positive impact on others and the world.
www.coffeebeankidsbook.com

Other Books by Jon Gordon

Printed and bound by CPI Group (UK) Ltd, Croydon, CR0 4YY

09/07/2026

14916217-0001